A ~~BITTER~~ BETTER END TIMES

There Is A Better Future Before
Jesus Returns

DR. DAN COFLIN

A Better End Times
Copyright 2024
Published by Coflin Family Publishing
ISBN: 978-0-9970643-3-9

Scripture quotations from the following sources:

Unless otherwise indicated, all Scriptures are taken from the *King James Version* of the Bible.

All Scripture quotations marked NKJV are taken from the *New King James Version* of the Bible. Copyright © 1979, 1980, 1982, Thomas Nelson, Inc., Publishers. Used by permission. All rights reserved.

The Scripture quotations marked CSB are taken from *The Christian Standard Bible*. Copyright © 2017 by Holman Bible Publishers. Used by permission. Christian Standard Bible® and CSB® are federally registered trademarks of Holman Bible Publishers. All rights reserved.

The Scripture quotations marked NASB are taken from the *New American Standard Bible*®. Copyright © 1960, 1971, 1977, 1995 by The Lockman Foundation. All rights reserved.

The Scripture quotation marked NIV is taken from the *Holy Bible, New International Version*®. Copyright © 1973, 1978, 1984, 2011 by Biblica, Inc.® Used by permission. All rights reserved worldwide.

The Scripture quotation marked TPT is taken from *The Passion Translation*®. Copyright © 2017 by BroadStreet Publishing® Group, LLC. Used by permission. All rights reserved. thePassionTranslation.com

The Scripture quotation marked AMP is taken from *The Amplified Bible*. Copyright © 2015 by The Lockman Foundation, La Habra, CA 90631. All rights reserved.

All scripture quotations in the publication are from the Contemporary English Version Copyright © 1991, 1992, 1995 by American Bible Society, Used by Permission.

NET Scripture quoted by permission. Quotations designated (NET) are from the NET Bible® copyright ©1996, 2019 by Biblical Studies Press, L.L.C. http://netbible.com. All rights reserved. Amplified Bible, Classic Edition. Works using Amplified Bible, Classic Edition quotations must include one of the following copyright notices (whichever one is most appropriate): 1. Scripture taken from the Amplified Bible, Copyright © 1954, 1958, 1962, 1964, 1965, 1987 by The Lockman Foundation. Used by permission

New Century Version (NCV) The Holy Bible, New Century Version®. Copyright © 2005 by Thomas Nelson, Inc.

New Life Version (NLV) Copyright © 1969, 2003 by Barbour Publishing, Inc.

Common English Bible (CEB) Copyright © 2011 by Common English Bible

Holman Christian Standard Bible (HCSB) Copyright © 1999, 2000, 2002, 2003, 2009 by Holman Bible Publishers, Nashville Tennessee. All rights reserved.

English Standard Version (ESV) The Holy Bible, English Standard Version. ESV® Text Edition: 2016. Copyright © 2001 by Crossway Bibles, a publishing ministry of Good News Publishers.

Expanded Bible (EXB) The Expanded Bible, Copyright © 2011 Thomas Nelson Inc. All rights reserved.

New Revised Standard Version, Anglicised (NRSVA) New Revised Standard Version Bible: Anglicised Edition, copyright © 1989, 1995 the Division of Christian Education of the National Council of the Churches of Christ in the United States of America. Used by permission. All rights reserved.

King James Version (KJV) – Public Domain

Young's Literal Translation (YLT) – Public Domain

Book Cover by April Robinson, Graphic Artist: apymarie@gmail.com
Text Design: Lisa Simpson: SimpsonProductions.net
Editing by: Paula Langhoff

Contents

Introduction 5

1. Context 9
2. The Son of Man Coming in the Clouds of Heaven 23
3. Signs of the End 33
4. How Long is a Thousand Years? 43
5. What About the Mark of the Beast? 67
6. Major World Events Following Jesus' Resurrection 83
7. The Book of Revelation.. 93
8. John's Vision of Heaven 105
9. Seven Trumpets 119
10. Signs in the Heavens 135
11. The Grapes Are Ready for Harvest 145
12. The Great Whore and the Scarlet Colored Beast 155
13. Satan is Bound, Loosed, and Destroyed 167
14. The Nature of Judgment 171
15. The Summary 181

Introduction

A Better End

WHAT IS YOUR WORLDVIEW?

What do you believe about the future of mankind?

How do you see our society in fifty years?

What do the terms "end times" or the "last days" mean to you?

Is your view of man's future on the earth one of hopeful anticipation, or of dread and fear of sorrow, pain, death, and annihilation?

The subject of "end time events" (eschatology) can be very confusing. I remember sitting in a church and listening to a well-known teacher on the subject. The year was 1972; I was eighteen years old and I truly knew nothing about the things he was teaching. I had not grown up in church, and much of the Bible was a mystery to me. I was born-again, but that was the extent of my scriptural knowledge.

As I sat in that pew for three or four nights listening to the terrible things that were about to happen on the earth; I was overwhelmed with a foreboding and much uncertainty about my future. Could these things be true? Was the world about to come to an end? This man seemed to be an expert on the subject, and taught as if there was no possibility of any other outcome.

Years later, many of these same ideas were taught in the Bible school I attended. Although the dates given by the man I had heard years before had come and gone and nothing that he said would happen actually happened; I was confronted again with the idea that we were at the end of days and the wrath of God was about to be poured out on the inhabitants of the earth.

This time, I was more familiar with the Scriptures that validated these prophetic ideas of coming disaster; yet some of the Scriptures seemed to be taken out of context or were referencing events that had already taken place, many centuries before. Again, I yielded to the experts and scholars, who obviously knew more about these things than I did.

As a young pastor, I was expected to know the Scriptures and be able to teach about all of the books of the Bible, including (of course), the *Book of Revelation*. Still unable to identify all of the types and symbols in these chapters; I resorted to a commentary written by a well-known teacher on the subject. As I launched out on the mission to teach this "scary" book, and following the commentary verse by verse, I was uncertain about the things I was teaching. Something just did not seem to fit, so I brought the series to a close and chose to avoid the subject in the future.

For years, this subject intrigued me as I listened to many different teachers, but they all were drawing the same conclusions from the same Scriptures, that to me, seemed to be taken out of context. I tried to accept these things, but something inside of me caused me to believe that something was still missing.

During this time, I "stumbled" across a book by John Bray, entitled *Matthew 24 Fulfilled*. As I read this book, I began to understand things from a different perspective. I did not know that there were any other "end time" positions but the premillennial, pretribulation Rapture of the Church just prior to a seven-year period of intense suffering and judgment; as the antichrist – possessed by the devil – takes over the world.

As one who loves history, I began to delve into the study of how the Church understood the *Book of Revelation* throughout the centuries, and discovered a number of different ideas and positions that were believed, and why. Preterist, historist, futurist, amillennial, and post-millennial are just a few of the many positions the Church has historically taken.

As I studied these beliefs and the history and Scriptures used to support them; I have come to the conclusion that our future here on planet earth is not "doom and gloom," but one filled with hope and the fulfillment of God's promise to cover the earth with the knowledge of the glory of God, as the waters cover the seas.

My hope is that you will lay aside any preconceived ideas you may have regarding the "end times" and what the *Book of Revelation* is really all about. I often tell my students that if you are going to rightly divide the word of truth, there are some things that are absolutely necessary to do when studying the Scriptures.

You should have the answers to the following questions:

- Who wrote the book?
- When was it written?
- What was happening at the time of the writing?
- Who is being addressed?

If you can answer these questions, you will be better able to put the Scripture you study into its proper context. After all, we are instructed to "rightly divide the word of truth" (2 Timothy 2:15).

If you cannot rightly divide or correctly teach the Word, then it is possible to teach incorrectly, get off course, be led astray, and lead others astray. James warns the Church to "let not many of you become teachers, knowing that we shall receive a stricter judgment" (James 3:1 NKJV).

It is my greatest desire to inspire you to revisit this subject that often seems confusing, and review these "end time" events in the light of both the Scriptures and the historical facts that have unfortunately been ignored all too often. I do not claim to have perfect understanding about all of the eschatological events as they are described in Scripture, but I have come to a better understanding of some of these things, and that causes me to have hope in a very bright future. Come along with me now, as we explore this fascinating subject.

Chapter 1

Context

When studying any biblical subject, it is extremely important to view every Scripture in its particular context. The word "context" carries the idea of "facts or circumstances that surround a situation or event." According to Webster's 1828 edition of the *American Dictionary of the English Language*, the word "context" means: "The general series or composition of a discourse…the parts of a discourse which precede or follow the sentence quoted…woven together or knit together."

In other words: if you want to understand what the author intended, you must take what is said in light of what precedes and follows the Scripture verse you are studying, in order to get the proper context or meaning of that Scripture.

When it comes to prophetic declarations about future events; it becomes extremely difficult to identify what the author intended, because right in the middle of talking about one thing, is another application of that Scripture that refers to something else.

Are you confused yet? Just stay with me. It's going to get better!

A good example of things being taken out of context is when Isaiah the prophet is talking to King Ahaz about a sign God wanted to give him. You see, Ahaz was the king of Judah and he was being threatened by the king of Israel and the king of Syria. God had sent the prophet Isaiah to Ahaz to tell him not to worry about those two kings, because within a very short time, they would both be destroyed.

Isaiah told Ahaz that God wanted to give him a sign to confirm that what he was hearing was true. When Ahaz refused, Isaiah said to him, "…the Lord himself shall give you a sign; Behold, a virgin shall conceive, and bear a son, and shall call his name Immanuel" (Isaiah 7:14).

The next several chapters of the *Book of Isaiah* tell us how Isaiah's wife conceived and bore a son who was the sign to Ahaz, that before the babe was old enough to know right from wrong, the two kings Ahaz feared, would be destroyed. We might be tempted to believe that the virgin who would bare a son named "Immanuel" was Isaiah's wife; but when we look at the *Book of Matthew*, we see that this "Immanuel" is Jesus (Matthew 1:22-23). Jesus was born some 700 years after Isaiah wrote this prophecy.

It seems that there is a pattern in Scripture, where someone is speaking; then suddenly, that person slips into a different realm and begins speaking prophetically about some future event. Their words do have relevance to the people they are speaking to, but often these same words carry a future spiritual fulfillment that refers to some event other than the time in which they are living.

King David wrote a psalm that could have referred to some of the many troubles he experienced. Here are a few of the things David said in this psalm:

"My God, My God, why have You forsaken Me"(Psalm 22:1 NKJV)?

"All those who see Me ridicule Me; They shoot out the lip, they shake the head, *saying*, 'He trusted in the LORD, let

Him rescue Him; Let Him deliver Him, since He delights in Him" (Psalms 22:7-8 NKJV)!

"For dogs have surrounded Me; The congregation of the wicked has enclosed Me. They pierced My hands and My feet"(Psalm 22:16 NKJV).

"They divide My garments among them, And for My clothing they cast lots"(Psalm 22:18 NKJV).

"His generation yet to be born will glorify him. And they will all declare, 'It is finished'"(Psalm 22:31 TPT)!

Now let's look at the gospels and see the fulfillment of the things David wrote some one thousand years earlier:

"My God, My God, why have You forsaken Me" (Matthew 27:46 NKJV)?

"Likewise also the chief priests mocking *him*, with the scribes and elders, said, 'He saved others; himself he cannot save…He trusted in God; let him deliver him now, if he will have him'" (Matthew 27:41-43).

"And they crucified him, and parted his garments, casting lots: that it might be fulfilled which was spoken by the prophet, They parted my garments among them, and upon my vesture did they cast lots" (Matthew 27:35).

"When Jesus therefore had received the vinegar, he said, It is finished" (John 19:30).

The psalm David wrote contains nearly direct quotes by Jesus, and those who stood around the cross observing these things. Did David know he was writing about events regarding the crucifixion of Christ? Most likely not, but he did write about things he knew nothing about. "Piercing" the hands and the feet describes crucifixion; however, crucifixion was not a practice in David's day. It came about many centuries later.

The context of this psalm that David wrote is easy for us to see, because Matthew describes the events of the crucifixion as the fulfillment of David's prophetic psalm (Matthew 27:35). It is much easier for us to put prophetic Scriptures into the proper context when the writers clearly identify an event as the fulfillment of the words of a particular prophet.

Peter stood up on the Day of Pentecost, after the 120 were filled with the Holy Spirit, and said to the multitudes, "But this is that which was spoken by the prophet Joel" (Acts 2:16). There was no question that the things Joel had prophesied centuries before were fulfilled in Peter's day.

Not all Scriptures have a prophetic fulfillment. Sometimes, Scripture simply states a spiritual truth.

Paul wrote to Timothy regarding the pastoral ministry and said, "Thou shalt not muzzle the ox that treadeth out the corn" (1 Timothy 5:18). He said this in reference to honoring the elders that worked in the church, by making sure they had provision to meet their needs. Paul was not likening the elders to oxen; but if it is right for the ox to eat of the grain he is grinding, then it is right for those elders who labor in the work of the ministry to also be fed.

Scriptures are not always meant to be translated literally because they may simply be a saying or an idiom.

For example, we say things such as, "Poor man; he jumped out of the frying pan and into the fire." Even this old English colloquial saying may not be understood by many of this current generation; but if we grew up hearing it, then we know what it means. But what if, five-hundred years from now, someone is reading an author who used this saying, and took them literally? This person might surmise that in our day, we had giant frying pans that people were being cooked in, and some jumped out of them and landed in the fire!

This person may develop a new system of belief that people in our day were cannibalistic. They might write in their history books about this torturous practice of our day; and yet, the simple truth is that this saying was not something anyone did, but only communicated to describe how some people go from one level of trouble to another.

Scriptures contain ideas that are sometimes represented by numbers, animals, trees, solar systems, or even articles of clothing.

Satan and wicked spirits are described as "snakes" and "scorpions." The animals Daniel saw in a dream represented kingdoms of nations; while the almond tree refers to a quick work of God, for the almond tree blossoms and produces fruit sooner than other trees.

In the *Book of Psalms*, it is recorded that God said, "Moab *is* my washpot; over Edom will I cast out my shoe" (Psalm 108:9). I'm sure many people are totally confused about what it means for God to cast out His shoe; but if we look in the *Book of Deuteronomy*, we find a statute where, if a man dies and leaves his wife childless, then the man's brother is to take his dead brother's wife as his own, and raise up children in the name of the dead brother (Deuteronomy 25:5-10).

If the brother refuses to marry her, then the widow is to go before the elders with her dead husband's brother. Then she is to loose his shoe from off of his foot, to publicly show that the man will not redeem his brother's widow by fathering children in the name of his dead brother. Although this practice may sound strange, the important thing for us is to understand what it means to "cast out your shoe." Simply speaking, God is saying that He will not redeem Edom as a nation for their wickedness because they oppressed Israel, their brother.[1]

Many times in Scripture, we see God's judgment on a nation described as "the sun and moon going dark" and "the stars falling from heaven." The "de-creation" (destruction) of a solar system (or its parts) represents God coming in judgment against the nations of Egypt, Babylon, Idumea, and Israel (Ezekiel 32:2,7-8; Isaiah 13:1,10; 34:4-6; Matthew 24:29). Just as the de-creation of a solar system represents God's judgment on kingdoms and nations; so is the discovery of a new star representative of the birth of a new king or kingdom.

When the Magi (an undetermined group of priests, astrologers, and astronomers) arrived in Jerusalem having come from the East (most likely Persia); the reason they gave for their visit was that they had seen a new star positioned over the land of Israel. To them, this meant that a new king had been born (Matthew 2:2).

With that news, King Herod consulted the scribes to see if the Scriptures identified the town where the Messiah would be born. Their search revealed that Bethlehem was the birthplace of the "ruler [of] Israel" (Micah 5:2).

---

[1] The Edomites were the descendants of Esau, Jacob's brother.

Both Herod and these "wise men" identified the presence of a new star to represent the birth of a new king. Kings and kingdoms are represented by stars or suns; and so is God's judgment on a kingdom or king revealed in the star (sun) being darkened. In other words, God is turning the lights out, and that kingdom will be destroyed.

Understanding symbols (something visible that represents something invisible or an idea) can be challenging unless we are told what the symbol represents.

When Joseph told his dreams to his father and brothers, they immediately understood their meaning (Genesis 37:5-11 NKJV). "There we were, binding sheaves in the field. Then behold, my sheaf arose and also stood upright; and indeed your sheaves stood all around and bowed down to my sheaf."

Joseph's brothers instantly understood the dream and replied, "Shall you indeed reign over us?" Joseph's next dream was also understood by his father. Joseph said, "Look, I have dreamed another dream. And this time, the sun, the moon, and the eleven stars bowed down to me." Joseph's father rebuked him, then asked, "What is this dream that you have dreamed? Shall your mother and I and your brothers indeed come to bow down to the earth before you?"

Joseph's father and brothers understood that in Joseph's dreams, they were represented first as sheaves; then as the sun, moon, and stars. His brothers were not sheaves or stars, and his father was not the sun, or his mother the moon, but the meaning of these symbols was understood.

There is no doubt that identifying the meanings of symbols in Scripture can be challenging. The *Book of Revelation* is a book of symbols. For centuries, scholars and church leaders, Catholic defenders, and protestant reformers have used the many symbols found in *Revelation* to promote their cause and explain that the events described in John's revelation were either an explanation of past historical events, or future prophecies yet to be fulfilled.

We find that the meanings given to the events and symbols in *Revelation* were often applied to the current events of the days that the commentators were living in. In times of peace and advancement of Christianity, many scholars took a post-millennial viewpoint.

Post-millennialism primarily views the events in *Revelation* as having been fulfilled in A.D. 70, when the Roman general Titus destroyed the city of Jerusalem and the Temple; and that John wrote about these things in the A.D. 60's, having been banished to the isle of Patmos under Nero's persecution. A "millennial" (1,000 years) is a representative period of time when believers are ruling and reigning with Christ, until all the nations of the earth are converted and discipled.

When the Church was going through times of great persecution and trouble, many church leaders took the position that they were in the end times and the Great Tribulation was soon to happen. They were looking for Jesus to return and rescue them from the demonic works of an antichrist; one who was some wicked ruler that was identified in many different lands and during different centuries.

In those times, the Church looked at the *Book of Revelation* from a pre-millennial viewpoint. This position sees the Apostle John's revelation as given to him while exiled on Patmos under Domitian's reign; and that all of the events in *Revelation* would take place at some future time when Jesus would return in judgment. In that day, He would destroy all of the wicked and resurrect the righteous; culminating in a 1,000-year period of time (millennial) when Jesus would rule the earth from a rebuilt Temple, in the city of Jerusalem.

These are just two of the many different understandings about "the Millennial" that the Church has embraced through the centuries. These "millennial" ideas are all derived from the twentieth chapter of the *Book of Revelation*, where a thousand-year time period is mentioned.

In 1517, Martin Luther nailed his 95 theses to the door of Castle Church in Whittenburg, Germany, in protest of many of the doctrines of the Catholic Church that he identified as unscriptural. The resulting conflict between Luther, the Pope, and other high-ranking church officials fostered a movement among many who agreed with Luther. Soon, the movement known as "The Reformation" would be in full swing in every European nation.

Luther and other reformers believed they were living in the time John described in the *Book of Revelation*, when the "antichrist" would arise and bring great persecution against the "true" church – the one represented by the reformers. Luther and others wrote volumes of commentary on Scripture and used the revelation of John to identify the Pope as the antichrist, who leads a corrupt and illegitimate church and spreads false doctrine and brings severe persecution against true believers.

This time of reformation closely followed the Renaissance (a cultural rebirth), when the nations of Europe came out of the dark ages and entered into a time of enlightenment. This was primarily initiated by the church establishing schools that taught people to read and write. This skill had been lost to the majority of people since the overthrow of the Roman Empire centuries earlier.

With the invention of the printing press and a literate populous, many could read for themselves what had previously been restricted to the priests, as the Scriptures were only written in Latin, which was no longer the language of the people.

The reformers translated the Scriptures into the language of the people; then wrote commentaries explaining that the days they were living in were described in the *Book of Revelation*. Multitudes began exiting the Catholic Church and began following the reformers. Martin Luther, Huldrych Zwingli, John Calvin, William Tyndale, and many of the reformers identified the Pope as the antichrist and warned the people to flee from the corrupt Catholic Church.

To challenge the reformers' viewpoint and to stop the hemorrhage of people from the Catholic Church, the Pope enlisted the help of the Jesuits. A Spanish Jesuit theologian named Francisco Ribera developed a 500-page commentary on the *Book of Revelation*.

He established a futuristic view of *Revelation*, showing that the antichrist was a single evil person outside of the established church, who would appear at the end of time, during a seven-year period of tribulation, just prior to the second coming of the Lord. He published his book in 1591. His view of the *Book of Revelation* became the official doctrine of the Catholic Church, and helped to reassure church members of the "heresy" of the reformers.

Years later, another Spanish Jesuit theologian, Emmanuel Lacunza, published a book in 1812, titled *The Coming of the Messiah in Glory and Majesty*. This book was built upon the futurist eschatological teaching of Ribera. Because it was published under

Lacunza's pen name, Ben-Ezra (who was supposed to have been a learned Jew who accepted Jesus as the Messiah), the book found its way onto the shelves of the library of the Archbishop of Canterbury in England. This book would have never been read by non-Catholics, if Lacunza had been identified as a Jesuit.

Edward Irving, a minister of the Church of Scotland, was greatly influenced by Lacunza's (Ben-Ezra's) book and had it translated into English. He added a 203-page preface to the book in 1827, and became a strong adherent to the futurist viewpoint. In turn, he greatly influenced two other men who followed Irving's teaching. These men were John Nelson Darby and Henry Drummond.

Darby was an Anglican minister who left the church to work with the Plymouth Brethren; and Drummond, who was a banker, founded the Catholic Apostolic Church. Together, these men, using Irving's writings, developed the belief that the return of the Lord would happen in two stages.

First, the Lord would return to catch away the saints before a time of great tribulation; and then Jesus would return at the end of the tribulation and resurrect the righteous dead to live with Him on the earth for a thousand years (millennium).

It is believed that their idea of the rapture of the church to rescue the saints prior to the Great Tribulation may have come from a prophetic word given by a young girl named Margaret MacDonald. This dispensational teaching became very popular during the last half of the nineteenth century because of a series of prophetic conferences that were held in England and the United States.

Another factor that greatly promoted this futuristic interpretation of end time events was the printing of the *Schofield Reference*

Bible and the *Dake's Annotated Reference Bible.* Both Cyrus Schofield and Finnis J. Dake embraced the teachings of John Nelson Darby and Henry Drummond.

The Schofield and Dake Bibles were the first to include detailed notes regarding the eschatological views presented by Darby and Drummond. These Bibles were greatly popular in most of the English-speaking nations of the world, and many times became a substitute for preparing pastors and other church leaders who may not have had the privilege of attending a formal Bible school or seminary. Therefore, this "end time" viewpoint was passed down to multiple generations by the teachings of those who followed the notes in these reference Bibles.

It is easy to see how Bible doctrines and people's world views can be developed because of the influence of a single teacher. That is why it is very important to understand the context of the verses, the historical settings they were written in and what is truly being referenced.

When Jesus was addressing the seven churches in Asia Minor (Turkey today), He was speaking of things that those hearing His words would understand. If He was really referring to Apache helicopters or computer chips, then the people He addressed would not have a clue about what He was talking about. No, Jesus' words addressed the people of that day.

Can we gain valuable information and understanding about spiritual things today by reading the words of Jesus to that generation? Of course, but we must realize that Jesus spoke to those seven churches specifically, using words they would understand.

We can see how important context is, to understand the meaning of any particular Scripture. We must also recognize that the

Scriptures are filled with signs and symbols that represent ideas, and that they are sometimes allegorical.

Paul uses Sara and Hagar and their respective children Isaac and Ishmael to represent the old and new covenants (Galatians 4:22-26). Here also, Mount Sinai, which represents the old covenant of the Law, is likened to the city of Jerusalem in Judea, which in Paul's day, was in bondage to the Romans.

New Jerusalem is a *heavenly* city and represents the new covenant, which is free from bondage; and represents all believers who have been born from above and are free from the Law. These people, mountains, and cities clearly represent the two covenants Paul was describing.

Now that we have discussed the importance of context, let's look at the return of the Lord and the destruction of the Jerusalem Temple.

Chapter 2

The Son of Man Coming in the Clouds of Heaven

"WHAT WILL BE THE SIGN of Your coming and of the end of the world?" This was the question the disciples asked Jesus when they were with Him in the city of Jerusalem (Matthew 24:3). To better understand the context of this question, let's review where they were and what Jesus had just finished saying.

Jesus had just left the Temple when His disciples came and wanted to show Him the buildings of the Temple. This statement may sound puzzling because Jesus had come to the Temple yearly since His childhood, but what they wanted to show Him was the new construction. King Herod had begun the building of this magnificent Temple forty-six years earlier, and the construction would continue for some thirty-six years after this time. It was this new construction that the disciples wished to show Jesus; something that obviously impressed the men.

They must have shown Him what was being built; but instead of Jesus commenting on the beauty of this amazing place, He said to them, "Do you see all these things? I tell you the truth, not one stone will be left on another. All will be torn down" (Matthew 24:2 NET)! The disciples must have been shocked at the words of Jesus, because they waited until He was alone to ask Him about when the destruction of the Temple would take place. They also asked about some of the things Jesus had taught when He was in the Temple earlier that day (Matthew 24:3).

Much of *Matthew 23* is a warning to the scribes, Pharisees, and religious leaders about the "woes" that would come upon them; culminating in a time of terrible judgment. Jesus declared that He would send to these religious leaders, prophets, wise men, and scribes, and that the leaders will not receive their word but would kill them, just like their ancestors killed the prophets of old.

This action by these corrupt leaders would soon bring upon themselves, a time of great tribulation and severe judgment that would be released upon that generation. This judgment would not only be for the blood of the righteous they would shed; but also for the blood of all the righteous shed upon the earth, going all the way back to the time when Cain slew his brother Abel (Matthew 23:34-35).

Can you imagine the severity of that kind of judgment? Jesus is saying that judgment for the blood of all the righteous shed upon the earth, from the very beginning of creation, would come upon that generation! Why would that generation be judged for the innocent blood that was shed thousands of years earlier? The answer may be found in the declaration that was made by the people who stood before Pilate at the trial of Jesus.

Remember that when the Jewish leaders had tried Jesus in their court, they found Him guilty of blasphemy. Then they brought Jesus before Pilate, the Roman governor, and demanded that he have Jesus crucified. Pilate quickly realized that the real reason the Jews wanted Jesus crucified was not because He had committed some crime, but because of envy.

Pilate attempted to release Jesus, knowing that He was innocent; but the threats of the mob finally caused Pilate to submit to their desires. But he first called for a bowl of water to wash his hands publicly, as he said to the crowd, "I am innocent of the blood of this just person" (Matthew 27:24). The next sentence declared by the people before Pilate's court is quite revealing: "Then answered all the people, and said, **His blood be on us, and on our children**" (Matthew 27:25).

Jesus came to shed His innocent blood to pay for the sins of all humanity for all time, but that generation would reject His sacrifice. As Jesus hung upon the cross and died, He willingly received the righteous judgment of God for the sin of man. He took man's place, dying as man's representative, and received the judgment of death God required for sin.

The blood of Jesus was shed for the purpose of forgiving mankind; however, that generation rejected the blood of Jesus for their sin, and cursed themselves by saying that the judgment for shedding His blood would rest upon them and their children— and that judgment would fall upon that generation.

A generation is typically identified in Scripture as forty years. Israel wandered in the desert for forty years, until "all the generation, that had done evil in the sight of the LORD, was consumed" (Numbers 32:13). Jesus had said that all these things that He had spoken of would come upon that generation (Matthew 23:33,36).

We also know that the number forty carries with it, the idea of trials, troubles, and tribulation. In the flood of Noah's day, it rained forty days and forty nights. Israel wandered forty years in the wilderness. Jesus was tempted by the devil as He spent forty days in the wilderness, and it was exactly forty years from the time Jesus made this declaration about God's judgment coming on that generation, until the time it was fulfilled in A.D. 70.

We might also remember Jonah's warning to the people of Nineveh, "Yet forty days, and Nineveh shall be overthrown" (Jonah 3:4). As God gave the inhabitants of the city of Nineveh forty days to repent before judgment would fall; God gave Israel forty years to repent. Unlike the Ninevites, Israel refused to repent, and the greatest tribulation recorded in the history of man fell upon that generation.

While I will not take the time here to detail the most terrible events during this time when Jerusalem fell, I would encourage interested readers to read the writings of Josephus, Suetonius, and Tacitus, regarding their records of these events.

Jesus' disciples asked Him about the sign of His coming and the end of the world, so how does His prediction of the destruction of the Temple and the city of Jerusalem answer their question? First, we need to understand that the phrase, "end of the world" is really the "end of the age." (The Greek word translated "world" here is *aion*, and means "age," not "world"). The disciples ask about when the end of the age would take place. Which age were they referring to?

Archaeologists identified the advancement of pre-historic peoples in ages, as the *Ice Age, Iron Age, Bronze Age,* etc. While I am quite certain the disciples of Jesus were not referring to these categories, since these ages would not be identified until centuries later; they recognized different ages in man's history, as recorded in the writings of the Old Testament.

They knew of the age from Adam to the flood of Noah's day. They were familiar with the age from Noah to Abraham and from Abraham to the giving of the Law under Moses. It was under Moses that the method of worshipping God changed from making sacrifices in the "high places" to only sacrificing upon the altar before the Tabernacle.

God's presence was known to be in the Tabernacle of Moses and then in the Temple built by Solomon. But the age of God dwelling in Temples made by man was coming to an end. Jesus had taught them that when the Spirit of God comes, He will live within them. Believers will be the new Temple of God; not a building made of stone.

Years later, the Apostle Paul would reiterate this truth to the Church in Corinth, when he said, "Do you not know that you are the temple of God and *that* the Spirit of God dwells in you?" (1 Corinthians 3:16 NKJV).

A time was coming that would usher in a new age when God would live in the very bodies of believers; and when there would be no more animal sacrifices on a man-made altar in a man-made Temple. Jesus was the Lamb of God, and His sacrifice on the cross was the only blood that could remove man's sin (Hebrews 9). The days of a Temple in Jerusalem and an altar for sacrifice were soon to be done away with. A new age was dawning, when God would live in man; and when the believers assembled (Church), there would be the Body of Christ.

As believers, we are individual members of the one and only Body of Christ. As members of His body, we are likened to *living stones* that make up a spiritual dwelling place (Temple) of God (1 Peter 2:5; Ephesians 2:20-22). The old system that contained observations of days, months, and years; and ordinances of sacrifices that the Temple in Jerusalem represented, was coming to an end.

We most often associate the "coming of the Son of Man in the clouds of heaven" to refer to the end of time when Jesus will return, but was that what Jesus was referring to? When Jesus came into Jerusalem with His disciples, He lamented of the city's future:

> O Jerusalem, Jerusalem, the one who kills the prophets and stones those who are sent to her! How often I wanted to gather your children together, as a hen gathers her chicks under *her* wings, but you were not willing! See! Your house is left to you desolate; for I say to you, you shall see Me no more till you say, "Blessed *is* He who comes in the name of the LORD" (Matthew 23:37-39 NKJV)!

Jesus warned the religious leaders of the total desolation of Jerusalem's house. It would be left uninhabited, a wasteland, and deserted. Jerusalem's house is either the Temple in the city or the city itself. Actually, both were utterly destroyed by the Romans in A.D. 70.

First century historians used the words of Micah the prophet to describe the utter destruction of the city, "Thus saith the LORD of hosts; Zion shall be plowed like a field, and Jerusalem shall become heaps" (Jeremiah 26:18). The Temple and the city of Jerusalem would be razed to the ground.

Following this warning of destruction, Jesus said they would not see Him anymore until they shall say, "Blessed *is* He who comes in the name of the Lord" (Matthew 23:39 NKJV). This statement by Jesus must be what His disciples were referring to when they asked Him, "What shall be the sign of Your coming? (Matthew 24:3 PARAPHRASED).

The Son of Man Coming in the Clouds of Heaven

I would like to give you an example that might help explain what Jesus was referring to when He told His disciples about the sign of His coming. I was born in the city of Tampa, Florida, and I have lived here all of my life. Over the years, the city has been visited by a number of United States Presidents. I have never seen a single one of them, but the signs they were here were undeniable.

Endless numbers of motorcades, the shutting down of roadways, literally hundreds of flashing lights, and traffic delays are all signs that the President has arrived. The President would travel by motorcade to a famous restaurant or to the house of a wealthy donor, where he would eat and address those in attendance. Most people would never see him, but the evidence of his presence was widely known.

I believe it was in this same fashion that Jesus said that He was returning to fulfill the judgment He had predicted upon the city of Jerusalem (and most notably) within that generation. Jesus said that they would not see Him again until they said, "Blessed is he that cometh in the name of the Lord" (Matthew 23:39).

So, did they physically see Jesus return in A.D. 70, or did they see the sign of His fulfilled word of judgment? Jesus said to Caiaphas, the high priest, "Hereafter shall ye see the Son of man sitting on the right hand of power, and coming in the clouds of heaven" (Matthew 26:64). Caiaphas was to see the words of Jesus fulfilled, and those words would confirm that Jesus was indeed that "Blessed One" that comes in the name of the Lord.

There are many Scriptures that declare that God comes in the clouds of heaven to fulfill the judgment declared by the prophets. The prophet Isaiah declared that "the LORD rideth upon a swift cloud, and shall come into Egypt" (Isaiah 19:1). The result of the Lord's coming into Egypt is described in the Scriptures that follow:

- The idols of Egypt shall be moved (Isaiah 19:1).

- The heart of the Egyptians shall melt (Isaiah 19:1).

- The Egyptians shall rise up against the Egyptians to fight their brothers, neighbors, city, and kingdom (Isaiah 19:2).

- The Egyptians will be given over into the hands of a cruel lord; and a fierce king shall rule over them (Isaiah 19:4).

This devastating destruction came to Egypt when Esarhaddon of Assyria ruled over them for nineteen years, with great cruelty. Do you think that the Egyptians physically saw the Lord riding upon a cloud, or was this prophetic language describing a work of God in the Spirit that would fulfill the word spoken by the prophet Isaiah?

Micah is another prophet whom God raised up to pronounce judgment upon Samaria and Jerusalem. He prophesied that the Lord would come out of His place, "and will come down, and tread upon the high places of the earth" (Micah 1:2-3). The Lord's coming would result in the mountains becoming "molten under him, and the valleys shall be cleft, as wax before the fire, and as the waters that are poured down a steep place" (Micah 1:4). The result of the Lord's coming would make Samaria "as an heap of the field: (Micah 1:6).

Again, this prophetic language describes what happened to Samaria after the Assyrian armies came and brought total destruction to that nation. Did the Samaritans see the Lord walking upon the melting mountains, or did they experience the fulfilled words of the prophet who used that imagery?

Becoming familiar with prophetic language helps us understand the imagery depicted in prophetic words. A few chapters later, Micah gives a prophetic word about a day when the "mountain of the house of the LORD shall be established in the top of the mountains, and it shall be exalted above the hills; and [all] people shall flow unto it (Micah 4:1).

Mountains and hills are often imagery of kingdoms and nations, so when the mountains of Samaria melt, we know the kingdom of Samaria is finished. In the same manner, the sign of Jesus coming in the clouds of heaven would be the devastation of the Temple and the city of Jerusalem. That judgment signified the end of the age of Temple worship and sacrifice.

Chapter 3

Signs of the End

How many times have you heard someone say, "Well, you know we are living in the last days and the signs of the times are all around us"? Usually, they are referring to what Jesus described in the twenty-fourth chapter of *Matthew*, and they equate that to the return of the Lord at the end of time. Is *Matthew 24* really referring to the end of time?

We have already looked at the coming of the Son of Man in the clouds and the end of the age, which refers to A.D. 70, when the Romans destroyed the Temple and the city of Jerusalem in fulfillment of the judgment Jesus said would come upon that generation. We need to remember that the disciples asked Jesus about the end of the "age," not the "end of time"; the end of the age was referring to the age of Temple worship and animal sacrifices according to the Law that Moses gave.

It is difficult for some people to hear the description of this judgment and apply it to the events of A.D. 70 when the Romans destroyed the Temple and the city of Jerusalem. "The sun being darkened and the stars falling from heaven" sounds as if these events would affect the whole of creation.

But the historical judgment of God on Egypt, Idumea, Babylon, Samaria, and other nations is described in the same fashion as Jesus described the judgment on the city of Jerusalem that was coming to that generation. All of these events would take place in "the last days" — between the resurrection of Christ in A.D. 30 and the destruction of the city and Temple in A.D. 70.

Many of the writers of the New Testament mentioned that they lived in "the last days." Peter, preaching to the multitudes in Jerusalem on the Day of Pentecost, declared that in that very day, the prophesy of Joel was fulfilled, "And it shall come to pass in the last days, saith God, I will pour out of my Spirit upon all flesh" (Acts 2:17).

The writer of *Hebrews* tells us that God's Son has spoken to us, "in these last days" (Hebrews 1:2). The Apostle John writes in his first epistle, "My dear children, these are the last days. You have heard that the enemy of Christ is coming, and now many enemies of Christ are already here. This is how we know that these are the last days (1 John 2:18 NCV).

The writer of *Hebrews* declares that the new covenant has come and that the old "is ready to vanish away" (Hebrews 8:13). Again, Peter writes regarding the coming of Jesus as our sacrifice, that He was "manifest in these last times for you" (1 Peter 1:20).

The last days or last times in these Scriptures are in reference to the end of the Old Testament age. Jesus ushered in a new age of grace; made possible because He was the final sacrifice for sin. The last days were in reference to those forty years between the resurrection of Christ (A.D. 30) and the destruction of Jerusalem and the Temple in A.D. 70.

What we need to understand is that there are Scriptures that refer to the coming of Jesus in judgment upon that generation, and that reference Jesus returning at the end of time (Matthew 23:36; 24:34).

Signs of the End

The "end of time" Scriptures are always associated with the resurrection of the dead. Jesus healed the lame man at the pool of Bethesda on the Sabbath day, and was challenged by the Pharisees for breaking the Sabbath day laws. As Jesus addressed these men who wanted to kill Him, (John 5:18) He said to them, "Verily, verily, I say unto you, The hour is coming, and now is, when the dead shall hear the voice of the Son of God: and they that hear shall live" (John 5:25).

Here, Jesus was speaking of that current time when those spiritually dead but physically alive people will hear His voice and receive spiritual life. Jesus then compares that to a future time when all that are in the graves (physically dead people) "shall hear his voice, And shall come forth; they that have done good, unto the resurrection of life; and they that have done evil, unto the resurrection of damnation" (John. 5:28-29).

This is in reference to a single day of resurrection when all physically dead people in the graves will hear the voice of Jesus and come out of the graves. Both the righteous and the wicked will be resurrected on that day.

In the very next chapter of *John*, Jesus is speaking to the crowds of people who had been fed bread and fish by Him and His disciples one day earlier. They returned to Jesus looking for more bread to eat. Jesus used that opportunity to teach them about the true "bread of life" (John 6:35). During that teaching, He referred to the physical resurrection He had mentioned in *John 5*. Let's look at these verses:

> "This is the will of the Father who sent Me, that of all He has given Me I should lose nothing but should raise it up at the last day. And this is the will of Him who sent Me, that everyone which sees the Son and believes in Him,

may have everlasting life; and I will raise him up at the last day" (John 6:39-40 NKJV).

"No one can come to Me unless the Father who sent Me draws him; and I will raise him up at the last day" (John 6:44 NKJV).

"Whoever eats My flesh and drinks My blood has eternal life, and I will raise him up at the last day" (John 6:54 NKJV).

Each of these verses of Scripture give us the time frame for the resurrection of the dead, and that is "the last day."

The Apostle Paul spoke of the resurrection when he wrote his first letter to the Corinthian Church. Here, he is teaching about the resurrection of Christ and how he is the "first fruits of those who have died" (1 Corinthians 15:20 NRSVA). Paul then begins to compare Adam and Jesus:

> For as in Adam all die, even so in Christ shall all be made alive. But every man in his own order: Christ the firstfruits; afterward they that are Christ's at his coming. Then cometh the end, when he shall have delivered up the kingdom to God, even the Father; when he shall have put down all rule and all authority and power. For he must reign, till he hath put all enemies under his feet. The last enemy that shall be destroyed is death" (1 Corinthians 15:22-26).

Jesus and others that were resurrected with Him are Christ and the "firstfruits" mentioned in the previous Scriptures (Matthew 27:52-53). Jesus fulfilled all the feasts of Israel, beginning with Passover (as the Lamb of God and sacrifice for sin), and then the Feast of Firstfruits, which is Sunday, the day after the Sabbath that follows Passover.

This is when the priests would go into the grain fields and harvest a few sheaves of the first ripe grain, and return to the Temple to wave the sheaves before the Lord. The first ripened grain was evidence of the promise of the full harvest that would follow.

Jesus and those who were raised up represented the firstfruits Paul mentioned. The rest of the harvest (resurrection) would take place at Christ's coming at "the end," when He shall deliver up the kingdom to God the Father, but that will not happen until He reigns and "he has put all enemies under his feet" (1 Corinthians 15:25).

I don't think anyone would challenge the fact that Jesus ascended to heaven after His resurrection and that He is sitting on the throne at the right hand of God the Father; ruling His kingdom from heaven (Ephesians 1:20-22; Colossians 3:1; Hebrews 8:1;12:2; Revelation 3:21). On second thought, I'm sure some people will not agree, but you can read the above Scriptures and decide for yourself.

From this heavenly position, Jesus is:

> ...far above all principality and power and might and dominion, and every name that is named, not only in this age but also in that which is to come. And He put all *things* under His feet and gave Him *to be* head over all *things* to the church, which is His body, the fullness of Him who fills all in all (Ephesians 1:21-23 NKJV).

So, Jesus reigns from heaven through His Church on the earth, which is His body. Some of the Church (His body) is now in heaven and some is on the earth, but there is coming a day when they shall all be gathered together (Ephesians 1:10).

What is Jesus waiting for? According to *Hebrews 10:12-13*; it is for His enemies to be made His footstool. This agrees with

Paul's declaration to the Ephesian Church that the Church is His body and that God put all things under His feet (the Church).

Again, in the *Book of Hebrews*, we are told that God has put all things under the feet of man, and that there is nothing that is not under man's feet. (If something is under your feet, it means you have authority over it) (Luke 10:19). The writer of *Hebrews* continues to say, "But now we see not yet all things put under him. But we see Jesus" (Hebrews 2:8-9).

The rest of this chapter continues to describe the work of Jesus to destroy the works of the devil; and deliver man from the bondage of sin and death.

God gave man authority and dominion in the earth beginning with Adam, but by Adam's sin, all of mankind came under the bondage of sin and death. Man was given authority, but now we don't see man walking in that authority as God ordained; however, we do see Jesus defeating the devil and delivering man to once again walk in the authority God gave him.

This is the commission Jesus gave to all of His disciples. They were to go into all the world, preach the gospel, disciple the nations, and establish the kingdom of God over all the earth; enforcing the defeat of every enemy Jesus has defeated, until all enemies have been put under His feet.

When will the end come and the resurrection of the last day take place?

...when he shall have delivered up the kingdom to God, even the Father; when he shall have put down all rule and all authority and power. For he [Jesus] must reign, till he has put all enemies under his feet. The last enemy that shall be destroyed is death (1 Corinthians 15:24-26).

What is the sign of the end before Jesus returns?

It will be when all His enemies have been put under His feet (the Church). Then, Jesus will return. There will be a resurrection of all of the dead on the last day, and Jesus will deliver up the kingdom of God to the Father and destroy death, the last enemy, forever. The signs of the end are not disasters and cataclysmic events, but the defeat of God's enemies.

Let me be quick to identify who are God's enemies; they are not people. God's love for mankind was perfect even when we were enemies (Romans 5:8-10). The enemies of God are those which steal, kill, and destroy (John 10:10). People may be used by the devil and wicked spirits to accomplish their evil purposes, but God's will for mankind is deliverance from the deception these evil spirits bring; and to bring every man, woman, and child into the kingdom of God.

When Paul was retelling the Roman authorities about his encounter with Jesus; he told them what Jesus had sent him to the nations to do:

> "To open their eyes, and to turn them from darkness to light, and from the power of Satan unto God, that they may receive forgiveness of sins, and inheritance among them which are sanctified by faith that is in me" (Acts 26:18).

This was Paul's assignment, and it is still the same for the Church today.

You may ask, "I thought you said that Jesus destroyed the devil. How come he is still active in the lives of people and nations today?" The answer to that question lies in the meaning of the word "destroy." The Greek word translated "destroy" here in *Hebrews 2:14* does not mean to "annihilate," but "to render entirely idle, useless, or unemployed."

There will come a day — the last day — when Satan is cast into a lake of fire, to be destroyed forever (Revelation 20:10). Until that time, we are to deal with him as the Apostle Peter described. "Be sober, be vigilant; because your adversary the devil walks about like a roaring lion, seeking whom he may devour. Resist him, steadfast in the faith" (1 Peter 5:8-9 NKJV).

The devil is unemployed and he is walking around trying to find someone to hire him, someone he can deceive and manipulate, to do what he wants. Unfortunately, there are many people who do not know who he is or what he does; as a result, he can work in them and through them. Some people do not yet know or believe the devil is real, or that Jesus has defeated him and has given them authority over him, yet God does not count them as His enemies.

Let us look at another Scripture that speaks to the timing of Jesus' return on the last day.

> And that He may send [to you] the Christ (the Messiah), Who before was designated *and* appointed for you–even Jesus, Whom heaven must receive [and retain] until the time for the complete restoration of all that God spoke by the mouth of all His holy prophets for ages past [from the

most ancient time in the memory of man] (Acts 3:20-21 AMPC).

This Scripture is part of the sermon that Peter was preaching to the multitudes, after healing the lame man at the gate Beautiful, at the Temple in Jerusalem. He tells us that, "heaven must receive [and retain]" Jesus until the restoration of all things that have been spoken by the prophets throughout the ages. As we look back to the prophets, there are many things that have been prophesied that have not yet taken place.

The prophet Isaiah speaks of a time in the "latter days" that "the mountain of the LORD's house shall be established in the top of the mountains, and shall be exalted above the hills; and all nations shall flow unto it" (Isaiah 2:2). Mountains and hills are often representative of kingdoms or nations.

This Scripture speaks of a time when God's kingdom is exalted above all other kingdoms, and all nations will come to God's kingdom; resulting in the people beating their "swords into plowshares, and their spears into pruninghooks" (Isaiah 2:4). Instead of warring against one another, the kings of the nations will use their military budgets for harvest.

The prophet Ezekiel speaks of a river that flows from the Temple of God, across the desert into the Dead Sea, and everywhere the river goes, it brings life to everything it touches (Ezekiel 47:1-9).

This sounds much like the river that is described in the last chapter of the *Book of Revelation,* that flows from the throne of God. Jesus identifies the river of God that flows from the heart of the believer to be the Holy Spirit; and from His abiding presence within the believer, flow "rivers of living water" (John 7:38).

Just as the river described in *Ezekiel* brings life and healing to everything it touches; so the believer who releases the river of God from within brings life to everyone who is touched by the Spirit of God. But there are those who are not touched by the river. They are described as "miry places" and "marshes" who will not be healed, but who are "given to salt" (Ezekiel 47:11).

So, not all nations or all people will come into the kingdom of God; neither will they experience the blessings of the kingdom, which includes righteousness, peace, and joy (Romans 14:17).

Some commentators assign the fulfillment of these verses to a time they refer to as "The Millennial reign of Christ." I will deal with this idea in the next chapter. For now, I hope you recognize that the "last days" have not lasted for two thousand years, but that they were fulfilled in A.D 70.

Chapter 4

How Long is a Thousand Years?

In previous chapters, I have already mentioned that numbers can represent ideas, and that they are not only limited to a single numerical value. There are many times that the numbers of days, months, or years described in Scripture are exact. We know that the inhabitants of the city of Jerusalem were in exile in Babylon for 70 years.

The prophetic declaration of Daniel was exact, when he said that when the command was given to rebuild the city of Jerusalem unto the coming of the Messiah, it would be 483 years. His prophetic word was fulfilled in exactly that time frame.

But there are times when numbers are mentioned that communicate an idea, not an exact numerical value. One of those times is when God spoke to His people and told them that "every beast of the forest is mine, and the cattle on a thousand hills" (Psalm 50:10). Was God saying that He only owned the cattle on a thousand hills, and the rest belonged to someone else? Well, of course not. We understand that God owns all the cattle on all the hills and that the number 1,000 represents *all*.

Scripture says, "Now, dear friends, do not let this one thing escape your notice, that a single day is like a thousand years with the Lord and a thousand years are like a single day"(2 Peter 3:8 NET). This is not a formula that adds a thousand years to every day, or that every thousand years represents a day. This is a reminder that God dwells outside of the realm of time, in eternity. He has no limits or expiration period; no beginning and no end. God knows all the ages that have been, and all the ages yet to come.

In this same passage of Scripture, Peter reminds those to whom he is writing, that in the last days (the days Peter lives in), there will be scoffers who will say, "Where is the promised return" (2 Peter 3:4 NET)?

The promise of Jesus' return in judgment upon that generation would be accomplished in forty years. During that time some of the "fathers" who had heard Jesus say these things died. Now their children are questioning if this judgment would ever happen.

> But as the days of Noah were, so shall also the coming of the Son of man be. For as in the days that were before the flood they were eating and drinking, marrying and giving in marriage, until the day that [Noah] entered into the ark, And knew not until the flood came, and took them all away; so shall also the coming of the Son of man be (Matthew 24:37-39).

Here, *Matthew* records the words of Jesus regarding His coming in judgment upon that generation. We know the time frame because in verse 34, He declares that the generation that was then living "shall not pass, till all these things be fulfilled," and that "Heaven and earth shall pass away, but my words shall not pass away" (Matthew 24:34-35).

Now, some teachers equate heaven and earth passing away as the end of the world, but remember that the phrase is prophetic language. We have seen it used many times, when referring to a kingdom, nation, or an age coming to an end. A new heaven and a new earth are not referring to a new physical earth or heaven, but "new heavens and a new earth, wherein dwelleth righteousness" (2 Peter 3:13).

In this same chapter in *2 Peter*, the scoffers are saying, "Where is the promise of his coming" (2 Peter 3:4)? These are the children of those who heard Jesus prophesying about His coming in judgment upon that generation. Peter mentions the previous age when the earth was overflowed with water and all but eight people perished.

That was Noah's flood that brought judgment upon all the inhabitants of the world in that age. Then there was a new heaven and new earth, "the heavens and the earth, which are now" (2 Peter 3:7). The "new heavens and earth" of that age – with a stone Temple and Old Covenant rituals and observances – are "reserved unto fire against the day of judgment and perdition of ungodly men" (2 Peter 3:7).

What will happen when the day of the Lord will come as a thief in the night?

"...the heavens shall pass away with a great noise, and the elements shall melt with fervent heat, the earth also and the works that are therein shall be burned up" (2 Peter 3:10).

What "elements" and "works" are meant here? The Greek word translated as "elements" is used seven times in the New Testament. Four of those times, the word is translated as "elements," and twice it is translated as "rudiments." In *Galatians* and *Colossians*, the term obviously refers to the operation of the Law of Moses in circumcision, offerings, the keeping of feasts days, and all things that have to do with keeping the Law (Galatians 4:3,9; Colossians 2:8,20).

Paul is speaking to believers in these churches, and challenging them not to return to the practice of the Law of Moses by these observances. The other two times this word is used is where the elements are melting with fervent heat; and speaks to the conflagration when the Temple and all its articles of worship are burning up (when the Romans destroyed the city and burned the Temple) (2 Peter 3:10,12).

The "heaven and earth" (this system of operation) of that age was being dissolved and destroyed; and the "new heavens and earth, wherein dwells righteousness" was being established. This new age of *grace* has a spiritual Temple, which is the body of believers; and the blood of Jesus is the only blood that can forgive sin and give righteousness (Hebrews 10:10-14).

The heavens and earth are often identified with prophetic language when describing judgment upon cities and nations.

Jeremiah laments over the destruction of Jerusalem and the cities of Judah in his day, and describes the results of that judgment:

> …the earth, and, lo, it was without form, and void; and the heavens, and they had no light…and all the cities… were broken down at the presence of the LORD, and by his fierce anger…For this shall the earth mourn, and the heavens above be black… (Jeremiah 4:23-29).

How Long is a Thousand Years?

Judgment on a corrupt city, nation, or system will produce God's work of righteousness as a new heaven and earth. God's judgment upon Jerusalem accompanied the fiery destruction of the Temple and the old covenant system of sacrifices. Now, the new heavens and earth God is in the process of creating are being established in the earth as His servants carry forth the gospel and disciple the nations.

This age of God's kingdom in the earth is often referred to as "The Millennial," or one thousand years. There are many different viewpoints regarding this thousand years. Is it literal, as an exact number of years, or is it symbolic for "all," as "the cattle on a thousand hills?" Through the years, scholars identify this thousand-year time frame as premillennial, amillennial, or postmillennial, and I'm sure someone somewhere has some other description for this time. A very elementary identification of these three millennial positions is as follows:

Premillennial – Jesus returns to the earth after a time of great tribulation (three and one-half years or seven years) and binds the devil for the thousand years; then He resurrects the righteous dead and rules from the physical city of Jerusalem in a rebuilt, man-made Temple, and all the resurrected righteous rule and reign with Him.

At the end of the thousand years, the devil is released from his prison and goes throughout the whole world, assembling the wicked who have not submitted themselves to the Lord. Then the devil brings this wicked army against the city of Jerusalem (where Jesus is); but in a moment of time, Jesus destroys all of the wicked and casts the devil into the lake of fire. Then all of the wicked dead are resurrected to stand in judgment before the throne of God, and God creates a new, physical heaven and earth.

Amillennial – This is literally "a," or non-millenarian, where one thousand years is symbolic. It identifies the beginning of the reign of Jesus in heaven; from His ascension until the successful subduing of all things unto Him, and His return to earth to resurrect all of the dead on the last day. Amillennialism centers on the reigning of the saints in heaven, with Jesus.

Post-millennial – This refers to the time of Jesus' return, "post" or after the Millennial. Again, this is a symbolic time frame that begins with the resurrection and ascension of Jesus. Jesus reigns from heaven, and the saints have dominion on the earth; as we have been spiritually "raised up with him and made to sit together with him in heavenly places" (Ephesians 2:6). The saints extend the kingdom of God throughout the whole earth, until "the earth shall be full of the knowledge of the Lord, as the waters cover the sea" (Isaiah 11:9).

Both amillennial and post-millennial positions are similar, in that they are *referencing* the thousand-year symbolism of time, and they focus on the "now" kingdom of God, as Jesus is reigning in heaven. Premillennialism describes the kingdom of God being established after His second coming and physical reign on the earth.

All three of these explanations are severely general; there are many different camps of understanding in each of these viewpoints that could be explored, but for brevity's sake, I will conclude with these definitions. A further explanation of Jesus binding the devil for a thousand years is helpful here. As we have considered in past chapters, we need to understand what Scriptures are referencing, whether something physical or spiritual.

In the *Book of Revelation*, we read that an angel comes down from heaven, with a key to the bottomless pit, and with a great chain in his hand. He binds the devil a thousand years and casts him into a pit to shut him up. Then, He sets a seal upon him so he cannot deceive the nations until the thousand years are fulfilled (Revelation 20:1-3).

Who is the "angel" that has keys and the authority to bind the devil? We need to understand that the word "angel" simply means "messenger." It does not always refer to a heavenly angel of God.

James reminds his readers about Rahab, and how she received the "messengers" (same word "angels") that Joshua had sent to Jericho (James 2:25). Jesus is also called the "messenger of the covenant" (Malachi 3:1); again, a Hebrew word also translated as "angel," one-hundred and eleven times in the Old Testament.

Jesus said that you can't enter the house of a strong man and spoil his house unless you first "bind the strong man" (Matthew 12:29). Who spoiled principalities and powers; triumphing over them? Jesus did (Colossians 2:15). As Jesus was about to accomplish His suffering for the redemption of mankind; God the Father spoke from heaven and Jesus said, "Now is the judgment of this world: now shall the prince of this world be cast out" (John 12:31).

Who has the keys of authority of death and hell? Jesus does (Revelation 1:18). Who destroyed the works of the devil? Jesus did (1 John 3:8). Jesus is the angel (messenger) that came down from heaven with keys of authority, and who bound the devil for a millennium so he cannot "deceive the nations" (Revelation 20:3). Jesus did not bind the devil with an iron chain, but with the Word of God; and He gives us the authority to do the same:

> ...I will give you the keys (authority) of the kingdom of heaven; and whatever you bind [forbid, declare to be improper and unlawful] on earth will have [already] been bound in heaven, and whatever you loose [permit, declare

lawful] on earth will have [already] been loosed in heaven (Matthew 16:19 AMP).

What is it that Jesus bound the devil from doing? From deceiving the nations (Revelation 20:3). As has been mentioned before, Jesus defeated death, hell, and the grave; He bound the devil, He was resurrected from the dead, He ascended into heaven, and is seated at the right hand of the Majesty on high. Jesus received all authority, power, and dominion; and sent the Holy Spirit to empower believers to carry the gospel to the people, and turn them from darkness to the light of salvation in Christ Jesus – and the devil can't do anything about it!

Some will say, "I thought we were going to be resurrected to rule and reign with Jesus during the Millennium?" Let us take a more careful look at who is reigning with Jesus, and when.

> And I saw thrones, and they sat upon them, and judgment was given unto them: and I saw the souls of them that were beheaded for the witness of Jesus, and for the word of God, and which had not worshipped the beast, neither his image, neither had received his mark upon their foreheads, or in their hands; and they lived and reigned with Christ a thousand years. But the rest of the dead lived not again until the thousand years were finished. This is the first resurrection (Revelation 20:4-5).

Before we get all tangled up with who the beast is, and what is the mark of the beast, let us look at the first resurrection. Resurrection is bringing back to life, something that was dead. We have already looked at what Jesus said in *John 5:25* about the dead who hear the voice of God and live. This verse speaks of those spiritually dead, but physically alive people who hear the Word of God and live, as a result.

Many Scriptures speak about those who are spiritually dead. "And you...who were dead in trespasses and sins..." (Ephesians 2:1) and "Even when we were dead because of our sins, He made us alive by what Christ did for us...God raised us up from death when he raised up Christ Jesus" (Ephesians 2:5-6 NLV). These verses of Scripture show us that before we came to Christ, we were spiritually dead; but after we received Christ, we were "quickened" or resurrected (made alive) (Ephesians 2:1,5).

John speaks of those who experience the first resurrection as those who did not worship the beast or his image, or receive his mark in their hands or foreheads. As a result of experiencing the first resurrection, the "second death" has no power over them.

What is John referring to when he says that the "second death" has no power over those who have experienced the "first resurrection?" What is the second death? To help us understand, let us look at the "first death" mentioned in Scripture.

When God placed man (Adam) in the Garden of Eden, He warned him not to eat of the "tree of the knowledge of good and evil," because if he did, he would experience death (Genesis 2:16-17). We know that Adam did eat of that tree. Although he lived physically for many years after that, he did experience a spiritual death (i.e. separation from God) on the day that he sinned.

Paul explains this, "For since by man came death, by man came also the resurrection of the dead. For as in Adam all die, even so in Christ shall all be made alive" (1 Corinthians 15:21-22). In verse 47, Jesus is called "the second man." Jesus, the second man, experienced the second death for all of mankind. He bore our sin and the judgment for our sin upon the cross.

Jesus died our death in our place, and reversed the curse of sin and death that had infected all of humanity. Because Jesus defeated death at the first resurrection, those who are in Jesus are not subject to the power of the second death, and are those who rule and reign with Him for a thousand years (Revelation 20:4-6).

Let us look at those who are ruling and reigning with Christ during the Millennium. The first group is those who are sitting on thrones and who have been given judgment (Revelation 20:4). Who are these rulers? When Peter asked Jesus about what he and the other apostles would receive for leaving everything and following Him, Jesus replied,

> And Jesus said unto them, Verily I say unto you, That [you] which have followed me, in the regeneration when the Son of man shall sit in the throne of his glory, [you] also shall sit upon twelve thrones, judging the twelve tribes of Israel (Matthew 19:28).

To understand this more fully, we need to know when Jesus, the Son of Man, shall sit on the throne of His glory. Here are some Scriptures that may help us:

> "Now of the things which we have spoken this is the sum: We have such an high priest, who is set on the right hand of the throne of the Majesty in the heavens" (Hebrews 8:1)

> "Looking unto Jesus the author and finisher of our faith; who for the joy that was set before him endured the cross, despising the shame, and is set down at the right hand of the throne of God" (Hebrews 12:2).

> "To him that [overcomes] will I grant to sit with me in my throne, even as I also overcame, and am set down with my Father in his throne" (Revelation 3:21).

> "Even when we were dead in sins, hath quickened us together with Christ, (by grace ye are saved;) And hath

raised us up together, and made us sit together in heavenly places in Christ Jesus" (Ephesians 2:5-6).

I believe the rulers who are sitting upon thrones and who have been given judgment are all the saints who have been born-again or have spiritually resurrected. Every believer has been given the "gift of righteousness" and is to "reign in life by one, Jesus Christ" (Romans 5:17).

We have been delivered "from the power of darkness" and have been translated, "into the kingdom of his dear Son" (Colossians 1:13). We are not waiting for the kingdom of God to start some day in the future; Jesus brought the kingdom of God with Him as He said when He came into Galilee, "preaching the gospel of the kingdom of God, And saying, The time is fulfilled, and the kingdom of God is at hand" (Mark 1:14-15).

When Jesus was disputing with the Pharisees, He said to them, "But, if I cast out devils by the Spirit of God, then the kingdom of God is come unto you" (Matthew 12:28). The kingdom of God is not in some geographical location (Luke 17:20-21), but is where "righteousness, peace and joy in the Holy Ghost" are ruling and reigning (Romans 14:17). When Jesus set someone free of the torments of a demonic spirit, *there* is the kingdom of God. When Jesus gave physical sight to someone who was blind, *there* is the kingdom of God.

So, when we are resurrected from spiritual death to spiritual life; we have received the power of the Holy Spirit and have been given the authority of the name of the Lord Jesus Christ to go and do the works of God that Jesus did (John 14:12). Then we are ruling and reigning in life, and functioning in the kingdom of God.

The second group described in *Revelation 20:4* is those who were "beheaded for the witness of Jesus, and for the word of

God." They also lived and reigned with Christ for a thousand years. Many people automatically assume that because they held the testimony of Jesus, that these must be New Testament saints who were born-again and who were martyred because they "lived and reigned with Christ a thousand years."

Therefore, they must have been physically raised from the dead. But there are several things we need to make note of, regarding the Old Testament saints: they knew of Jesus long before He was born in Bethlehem.

> Your father Abraham rejoiced to see my day: and he saw it, and was glad. Then said the Jews unto him, Thou art not yet fifty years old, and hast thou seen Abraham? Jesus said unto them, Verily, verily, I say unto you, Before Abraham was, I am. (John 8:56-58).

Of Him, all the prophets bear witness that through His name, everyone who believes in Him receives forgiveness of sins (Acts 10:43). But now apart from the Law, the righteousness of God has been manifested, being witnessed by the Law and the Prophets, even the righteousness of God through faith in Jesus Christ, to all and on all those who believe (Romans 3:21-22).

These few Scriptures —and there are many more — reveal that the Old Testament prophets prophesied about Jesus and the salvation He would bring. Many of these Old Testament believers were martyred in various ways.

The *Book of Hebrews* (Hebrews 11:35-39) tells us that they were stoned, sawn in two, slain with the sword. Even John the Baptist, whom Jesus called the greatest prophet of the Old Testament, was beheaded by Herod Antipas (Matthew 11:11; 14:1-12). So, just because these martyrs held the testimony of Jesus, it did not mean that they lived in the age of the New Testament.

They were not born-again or went to heaven until after Jesus died on the cross and completed the work of redemption. Jesus said that no man had ascended into heaven except the Son of man that came down from heaven (John 3:13). Until Jesus had paid the price for our sin upon the cross, no one went to heaven when they died.

In the story of the rich man and the beggar Lazarus, we learn that the beggar died and was carried by the angels to "Abraham's bosom." A rich man also died; in Hades, he looked up and saw Abraham "afar off," and Lazarus in his bosom (Luke 16:22). The story continues to reveal to us that the place of the righteous dead was not in heaven, but in "paradise" or "Abraham's bosom," in the "lower parts of the earth" – until after Jesus arose from the dead.

The Scriptures tell us that Jesus "ascended, what is it but that he also descended first into the lower parts of the earth? He that descended is the same also that ascended up far above all heavens, that he might fill all things" (Ephesians 4:9-10). Peter also tells us that after Jesus died on the cross, He "went and preached to the spirits in prison" (1 Peter 3:19).

No one else could breach the great gulf that separates the righteous dead from the wicked dead, except Jesus, who, "When he ascended up on high, he led captivity captive" (Ephesians 4:8). Jesus led the righteous souls of those who were held captive in paradise, out of captivity when He rose from the dead and ascended into heaven.

There were many Old Testament saints that were killed for their testimony and who were awaiting the arrival of the Messiah (Savior) to take them to heaven, where they too would rule and reign with Jesus.

Of course, many New Testament saints martyred for their faith ascended to heaven, like Stephen, who saw Jesus, "standing on the right hand of God," ready to receive him (Acts 7:56). This is confirmed by Paul, who said, "to be absent from the body" is "to be present with the Lord" (2 Corinthians 5:8).

These Old Testament saints were not physically resurrected after Jesus led them out of paradise and into heaven; however, some came out of the graves at the resurrection of Jesus and walked through the streets of Jerusalem, appearing to some of the people (Matthew 27:52-53). These were part of the "firstfruits" who were resurrected with Jesus (1 Corinthians 15:20-21). Everyone else will be resurrected at the coming of Jesus, at the end of time.

It may help us to understand both the position and the condition of the saints, whether they are here on the earth, or have gone on to heaven. Everyone who has been born-again of the Spirit of God has a position of being seated at Jesus' right hand, to rule and reign with Him.

The current condition of the saints is that some are in heaven, and some are on the earth. The promise of the Word of God is that there will come a time when God will, "gather together in one all things in Christ, both which are in heaven, and which are on earth" (Ephesians 1:10).

Until that time, God has "raised us up together with him and seated us together with him in the heavenly realms in Christ Jesus" (Ephesians 2:6 NET). As members of the body of Christ, it does not matter if we are still physically alive on earth, or if we have physically died and gone to heaven; our condition is different but our position is the same.

This is probably a good place to mention that when you go to heaven, you are not on some kind of eternal vacation. Just because you change locations does not mean that your purpose no longer exists. You may not be employed in the kind of activities you functioned in on the earth; but you did not cease to be a member of the body of Christ or to have a purpose or assignments or responsibilities.

There may be no need for bank tellers, schoolteachers, policemen, or attorneys in heaven, but the few glimpses of heaven we see in the Scriptures shows us that people there are busy. There are multitudes worshipping God and there are individuals assigned to certain tasks.

Twice in the *Book of Revelation*, John is having certain things revealed to him by an angel. We have already seen that angels are sometimes heavenly beings, and sometimes people are called "angels," because the word simply means "messengers."

In John's experience, an "angel" told him to write certain things that he told him. When John heard him speak, he fell at the feet of the angel (messenger) to worship him. The angel responded by saying, "Don't do this! For I am only a fellow servant with you and one of your brothers who clings to what Jesus testifies" (Revelation 19:10 TPT).

It may not be absolutely clear, but it appears that this was a human messenger, and not an angelic being that had the assignment of bringing John a message. (This action of John and response of the angel is repeated in *Revelation 22:8-9*). Obviously, if we are ruling and reigning with Christ, we have responsibilities to fulfill, whether we are here on earth or in the heavenly realm.

So far, in the twentieth chapter of the *Book of Revelation,* we have seen that an angel (Jesus) comes down from heaven, and that He binds the devil from deceiving the nations for a thousand years. Again, metaphorically speaking, this is not necessarily a definite period of time. Then John sees thrones, and those who sit upon them, ruling and reigning with Christ (a function of the saints both in heaven and earth). Then we are told, "the rest of the dead lived not again until the thousand years were finished. This is the first resurrection" (Revelation 20:5).[2]

We have already identified those who have been part of the "first resurrection" as those who have been born-again and who have resurrected to spiritual life from spiritual death. The saints who physically die are present with the Lord ("to be absent from the body is to be present with the Lord") (2 Corinthians 5:8). Their physical bodies are in the grave, but their spirits and souls are with the Lord.

Those who are spiritually dead and who die physically have bodies in the grave, but spirits and souls in the realm of "death and hell" (Revelation 20:13). Death and hell (Hades, the place or state of departed souls) release the dead that are in them, to stand before the "great white throne" and be judged according to their works, after the thousand years are over. This fits perfectly with Jesus' statement regarding the physical resurrection of the dead:

---

[2] This phrase, "the rest of the dead lived not again until the thousand years were finished" may or may not have been included in the original text. The *Codex Sinaiticus*, believed to be the oldest and most complete and accurate Greek text prior to the fifth century, does not include this phrase. Neither does the Aramaic New Testament, translated into English from the Peshitta text. It is believed that scribes sometimes wrote notes next to the verses that were made by the copyist; and over the course of time, some of these notes were absorbed into the text itself. Verse 5 in both the Aramaic and Sinaitic texts simply says, "This is the first resurrection." If this phrase is included, then who are the dead? These could not be the spiritually dead but physically alive, because they could become converted and made part of the first resurrection. If they are physically dead, then they would be part of the general resurrection of all people at the last day.)

...the hour is coming, in the which all that are in the graves shall hear his voice, And shall come forth; they that have done good, unto the resurrection of life; and they that have done evil, unto the resurrection of damnation" (John 5:28-29).

I realize there is much debate about eternal judgment. Are all those who stand before God judged according to "their" works, or according to "His" works (i.e. what Jesus did)? There are obvious rewards for good works (silver, gold, and precious stones), and loss for works of no value (wood, hay, and stubble, as seen in *1 Corinthians 3:12-15.*

Did the sacrifice of Jesus upon the cross pay for the sins of all humanity; even those who have never heard the gospel? Is it necessary to hear, believe, and receive the gospel in order to be saved? All of these are legitimate questions that the Church has debated for years. My purpose here is not to debate the meaning of eternal judgment, but to identify the "first resurrection" as spiritual, and the "physical resurrection" of the last day."

When will this resurrection of the wicked and of the righteous take place? According to Jesus, it will be on the "last day." Over and over, Jesus talks about raising up the righteous on the "last day" (John 6:39-40,44,54). Our question then, is on the last day of *what*?

We have already looked at the different "ages" in the Bible. These "ages" are accompanied by "a new heaven and earth." After the flood, in the days of Noah, a new age began, with a new heaven and earth that was purged by the flood. And the age of the stone Temple in Jerusalem and of the blood sacrifices on the brazen altar came to an end with the physical death, burial, and resurrection of Jesus; whereby we entered into a new age of grace.

The Lord gave Israel forty years to repent and embrace this new covenant; but at the end of those forty years, a great judgment came upon the city of Jerusalem, that resulted in the destruction of the Temple. In the description of that judgment, the old "heaven and earth" was destroyed and the new (where righteousness dwells) came into being.

Once again, at the end of the 1,000 years (Millennial), the "earth and heaven fled away" (Revelation 20:11) from the face of Him who sits upon the great white throne. This occurs at the last day, when the Lord returns with His saints to witness the opening of the graves and the transformation of those who are still physically alive and who receive their glorified bodies (1 Corinthians 15:51-52; 1 Thessalonians 4:14-17).

The wicked dead are also resurrected, as Hades gives up the dead that are there, to stand before the Lord in judgment. It seems that this will all be accomplished on "the last day" of this age; when all enemies have been put beneath the feet of Jesus (the body of Christ) – when Jesus physically returns from heaven to deal with the last enemy called death (1 Corinthians 15:26).

At the end of the Millennial age (1,000 years), Satan is loosed from his prison (Revelation 20:7). This may be on the last day or near the last day of this age. Satan is loosed from what he was bound from doing, which was deceiving the nations. The purpose of Satan being loosed is to gather those unbelieving nations to battle against the camp of the saints of God and the beloved city. Here, the wicked nations are seen surrounding the "camp" or castle, compound, or barracks of the saints, and the beloved city.

What is pictured here is reminiscent of Ezekiel's description of Israel's battle with Gog and Magog (Ezekiel chapters 38-39). Ezekiel's prophecy depicts the Maccabee's defeat of the Syrians in the second century B.C., just as God destroyed the Syrian invaders who were intent on annihilating the people of God. In the same way, God will supernaturally destroy Satan's hordes when they come to fight against the saints.

The "beloved city" is not old Jerusalem that suffered the judgment of God, but the new or heavenly Jerusalem described in *Hebrews 12:*

> But [you] are come unto mount Sion [Zion], and unto the city of the living God, the heavenly Jerusalem, and to an innumerable company of angels, [to] the general assembly and church of the firstborn, which are written in heaven, and to God the Judge of all, and to the spirits of just men made perfect, [and] to Jesus the mediator of the new covenant, and to the blood of sprinkling… (Hebrews 12:22-24).

This "beloved city" is described in great detail in the next chapter of *Revelation,* but here are some things we can understand about this city:

It is seen at the beginning of a new age (Revelation 21:1). There is a new heaven and a new earth, which we have already determined to be a description of a new age.

It comes from God out of heaven as a bride and is described as the Lamb's wife (Revelation 21:2,9-10). This city is adorned as a bride. When the angel showed John the bride (the Lamb's wife), John saw the great city, holy Jerusalem.

The city is described as a precious stone that has twelve gates and twelve foundations made of precious stones. The gates and foundations are inscribed with the names of the twelve tribes of Israel and the twelve apostles of the Lamb (Revelation 21:11-14,19-20).

Believers are described as stones of a building that is built upon the "foundation of the apostles and prophets, Jesus Christ himself being the chief corner stone...[and] all the building [is] fitly framed together...for a habitation of God through the Spirit" (Ephesians 2:20-22). "[You] also, as [living] stones, are built up a spiritual house" (1 Peter 2:5).

Both the gates and the foundations of the city have the names of the twelve tribes of Israel and the twelve Apostles of the Lamb inscribed upon them (respectively). The significance of the number twelve is seen throughout the Bible. Most Bible commentaries agree that the number twelve is indicative of the government of God or the people of God.

In the Old Testament, the people of God were identified as the twelve tribes of Israel. In the New Testament, it is the twelve Apostles of the Lamb who are the spiritual foundations for the building of the Church (Ephesians 2:20).

When we see twenty-four elders sitting on twenty-four thrones around the throne of God, we are seeing a representation of all of the Old Testament and New Testament saints (Revelation 4:4). When John heard the number of those who were sealed in their foreheads (144,000), we understand that this is, again, a representative number of all of the people of God (12,000 times 12). John heard this number and turned and saw, "a great multitude, which no one could number" (Revelation 7:4-9).

The city is a cube or foursquare (Revelation 21:16). The city is a cube. It is as long as it is wide and as high. Each side of the cube is 12,000 furlongs or stadia. Sometimes, different translations measure the city by the measurements they believe to be equal to a "stadia." Therefore, they interpret the measurement as 1400 or 1500 miles; but the significance is not found in the physical length of the measurement, but in the representative number of 12,000. Again, this number is symbolic for all of the people of God.

It is interesting that the only other place we find a cube in Scripture, is in the "most holy place" (1 Kings 6:19-20). This "most holy place," sometimes referred to as the Holy of Holies, is where the Ark of the Covenant was placed in the innermost part of the Temple, where God dwells. Toward the end of this chapter, it is mentioned that John saw no Temple in the city, "for the Lord God Almighty and the Lamb are the temple of it" (Revelation 21:22).

The city has no Temple because the Lord God Almighty and the Lamb are the Temple (Revelation 21:22). Now when John sees the bride (the New Jerusalem), he sees the angel with a reed, who measures not the Temple – for God Himself is the Temple of this city – but the city itself. Once again, we see the dimensions of this city as a cube: 12,000 stadia; and the wall surrounding it is 144 cubits (12 x 12), representing the people of God.

The city has no need for sunlight because the glory of God lightens it (Revelation 21:23). This city had no need of the sun, because "the glory of God lights it up, and its lamp is the Lamb" (Revelation 21:23 NET). This is reminiscent of the description given in the *Book of Genesis* about the first day of creation, when the earth was dark. "And God said, Let there be light: and there was light" (Genesis 1:3).

This light was obviously not the light of the sun, because it was not until day four that we see the sun, moon, and stars of heaven created. So, the light seen on day one in *Genesis* must be the same light described as the glory of God in *Revelation*.

Jesus said, "I am the light of the world" (John 8:12). John writes, "In the beginning was the Word, and the Word was with God, and the Word was God. The same was in the beginning with God. All things were made by him; and without him was not [anything] made that was made...And the Word was made flesh, and dwelt among us (and we beheld his glory, the glory as of the only begotten of the Father,) full of grace and truth" (John 1:1-3,14).

Revelation 21 also mentions the nations and kings of the earth, who bring their glory and [honor] into this city of God. The gates of the city are always open, but nothing can enter the city that would defile. Only those who are "written in the Lamb's book of life" can enter the city (Revelation 21:24-27).

Repeatedly, we see prophetic words that speak of the kings and kingdoms of the earth, who submit themselves to the "KING OF KINGS, AND LORD OF LORDS" (Revelation 19:16). Isaiah declares, "And it shall come to pass in the [latter] days, that the mountain of the LORD's house shall be established in the top of the mountains, and shall be exalted above the hills; and all nations shall flow unto it" (Isaiah 2:2).

Daniel interprets the dream king Nebuchadnezzar had, when he saw an image of a man that was made of different elements: gold, silver, brass, iron, and clay. A stone fell on the image, and broke it into tiny pieces, that the wind blew away. Then the stone grew to become a great mountain that filled the earth.

In Daniel's explanation, the parts of the image that were made of different elements represented both the current kingdom of Daniel's day (Babylon), and the coming future kingdoms, representing the Medes and Persians, Greeks, and Romans. In the day of the Roman kingdom (Empire), a stone would crush the image and then grow to become a great mountain. This stone is Jesus and this mountain is the kingdom of God (Daniel 2:27-45).

This same theme is often repeated in the Scriptures. Isaiah speaks of the glory of God that will arise upon His people; the result will be that the kings of the nations will bring their wealth to the city of God.

> Arise, shine, for your light has come, and the glory of the LORD shines over you...Nations will come to your light, and kings to your shining brightness...I will glorify my beautiful house...Your city gates will always be open; they will never be shut day or night so that the wealth of the nations may be brought into you, with their kings being led in procession (Isaiah 60:1,3,7,11 CSB).

These Scriptures and others like them are usually applied to a Millennial reign of Christ, after He returns and dwells in a rebuilt stone Temple in the land of Israel. But Jesus is the one who is building His "Church" (Matthew 16:18), which is His Temple (1 Corinthians 3:9-16); and the glory of the Lord has been given to His disciples (John 17:22).

Paul said, "Howbeit that was not first which is spiritual, but that which is natural; and afterward that which is spiritual" (1 Corinthians 15:46). Jesus now has a spiritual Temple. He is not going backward to live in a man-made stone Temple.

Notice that in *1 Corinthians,* Paul is speaking of building on the only true foundation (Christ), and the elements of this spiritual Temple that will abide the test of God's glory: silver, gold, and precious stones (1 Corinthians 3:11-13), just like the Temple described in *Revelation 21*.

Chapter 5

What About the Mark of the Beast?

MOST PEOPLE HAVE HEARD DIFFERENT ideas about the "beast" and the "mark of the beast," on the hand and forehead of those who worship the beast and his image.

Back in the days when Ronald Regan was the President of the United States, I heard many teachers of the "end times" say they believed that Mikhail Gorbachev was the beast, whom they equated to the antichrist; and that the strange birthmark on his forehead was proof.

The reasoning was that he was the leader of the Soviet Union, and there was speculation of a nuclear war, where America would be destroyed and the Soviets under Gorbachev would take over the world and persecute the Church. Of course, not long after that, the Soviet Union collapsed and Gorbachev was no longer in power.

Prior to Gorbachev's time, some teachers identified Henry Kissinger as the antichrist and beast. Mr. Kissinger was the U.S. Secretary of State and National Security Advisor under President Richard Nixon. This accusation resulted from the numerical numbers that were derived from the letters of his name adding up to 666, using the Gematria of Jewish culture (a numbering system of older origin).

This same dubious system and summation have been used to similarly identify countless people in leadership. Using the Greek or the Hebrew alphabets, people look for numerical connections to a potential candidate who will become this ultimate evil ruler; often based solely upon the numerical value of the letters of their names. If we look further back in history, we find that five-hundred years ago, it was the reformers who identified the leader of the Catholic Church (the pope) to be this same evil beast.

To get a clearer understanding of who or what the antichrist is; we should look at Scripture, and not the current events of our day to make such a determination. First, the term "antichrist" is not found anywhere in the *Book of Revelation*. It is found only five times, and each of these mentions are found in John's epistles, as we see in the following Scriptures:

> Little children, it is the last time: and as [you] have heard that antichrist shall come, even now are there many antichrists; whereby we know that it is the last time. They went out from us, but they were not of us: for if they had been of us, they would no doubt have continued with us: but they went out, that they might be made manifest that they were not all of us (1 John 2:18-19).

> And every spirit that [confesses] not that Jesus Christ is come in the flesh is not of God: and this is that spirit of antichrist whereof [you] have heard that it should come; and even now already is it in the world. [You] are of God, little children, and have overcome them: because greater is he that is in you, than he that is in the world (1 John 4:3-4).

"For many deceivers are entered into the world, who confess not that Jesus Christ is come in the flesh. This is a deceiver and an antichrist" (2 John 1:7).

Notice that John says that "it is the last time." John is speaking about the "last days"; regarding the time in which he was living, until the fulfillment of the words of Jesus, when the city of Jerusalem and the Temple would fall in that generation. We also see that there are "many antichrists" and that they "went out from us."

Apparently, they were in the Church, but they went out from the Church to make manifest that they "were not of us." These "deceivers" do not confess that Jesus Christ came in the flesh (a doctrine of the Gnostics of John's day); and that the Church had overcome them (antichrists) because the greater one (Jesus) lived in them (the Church).

The term "antichrist" means "instead of" or "in opposition to Christ." We might find that spirit in the *Book of Revelation*, but not that terminology; even though John was the writer of both the epistles and the *Book of Revelation*. What we do find in the *Book of Revelation* are beasts. A beast rises out of the bottomless pit, a beast rises out of the sea, and a beast rises out of the earth; so there are different beasts, and they resemble a leopard, a bear, a lion, and a lamb (Revelation 11:7; 13:1-2,11).

It is interesting that this is not the first time we see these beasts in Scripture. In the first year of King Belshazzar (the last king of Babylon), the prophet Daniel had a dream about four beasts: a lion, a bear, a leopard; and a fourth beast that was diverse, terrible, dreadful, and exceedingly strong, with great iron teeth (Daniel 7:1-7). The chapter continues to describe these beasts as kingdoms; and certain kings that ruled these kingdoms and that oppressed the people of God.

Also associated with the fourth kingdom were ten horns. Among them was a "little horn," with eyes like a man and a mouth speaking great things (Daniel 7:8). Later in this chapter of *Daniel*, the beasts, the horns, and the little horn that "made war with the saints" for three and one-half years are explained (Daniel 7:19-21,24-25).

First, let's look at these four beasts or kingdoms. The *Book of Daniel* gives many references to the four kingdoms of man, from the time of Daniel to the coming of Christ. This begins with King Nebuchadnezzar's dream of an image with a head of gold, breasts and arms of silver, a belly and thighs of brass, legs of iron, and feet of iron and clay (Daniel 2:31-33). Daniel interprets the meaning of this dream as representing four kingdoms. And in the time of the fourth kingdom, a stone will fall upon and crush the image (kingdoms) and then grow to become a great mountain that fills all the earth.

Because Daniel identifies the current Babylonian kingdom as the first of these four kingdoms, it is not difficult to identify the others. Following the Babylonian Empire was the Medo-Persian Empire; then the Greek Empire, followed by the Roman Empire. So, it was in the days of the Roman Empire that a stone would fall on and crush the empires of man (the kingdoms of the world); and grow to be a great mountain that fills the whole earth. Jesus is identified as "The stone which the builders rejected, the same is become the head of the corner" (Matthew 21:42).

It was in the days of the fourth kingdom (the Roman Empire) that Jesus came, and whom the religious leaders rejected. He became both the foundation and the cornerstone of the spiritual Temple (the Church) that He is building. The stone grew to become a great mountain that filled the whole earth.

What About the Mark of the Beast?

We have already looked at the significance of mountains representing kingdoms. Here, the mountain (kingdom of God) grown from the stone (Jesus), shatters all other kingdoms and is what fills the whole earth. The "kingdoms of this world have become *the kingdoms* of our Lord and of his Christ" (Revelation 11:15 NKJV). So, we see that this image represents four world empires or kingdoms, just as the four beasts do in *Daniel 7*.

Looking again at the seventh chapter of *Daniel*, it was in the days of the fourth beast (Rome) that we see that "thrones were set up, and the Ancient of days (God) took His seat" (Daniel 7:9 AMP). This portion of Scripture goes on to reveal the Ancient of Days in the same way we see Jesus described by John, "…one like unto the Son of man…His head and his hairs were white like wool, as white as snow; and his eyes were as a flame of fire…and his voice as the sound of many waters" (Revelation 1:13-15).

Daniel continues to say, "…the Son of man came with the clouds of heaven, and came to the Ancient of Days, and they brought him near before him. And there was given him dominion, and glory, and a kingdom…an everlasting dominion…and his kingdom that which shall not be destroyed" (Daniel 7:13-14).

Daniel is revealing events that Jesus would fulfill. Just before Jesus ascended to heaven from the Mount of Olives, He told the five hundred who had assembled there, to wait in the city of Jerusalem until they were filled with the Holy Spirit (Acts 1:4-9; Matthew 28:18-20). Those saints would carry the gospel of the kingdom to the ends of the earth.

That was the beginning of the kingdom of God filling the earth. This work is still going on today, and will continue until Jesus returns; after He has accomplished, through His Church, the work of putting all enemies under his feet (1 Corinthians 15:24-27; Ephesians 1:22-23).

What about the "little horn?" The seventh chapter of *Daniel* continues to explain the events that were to transpire during the time of the fourth kingdom (Rome). While we may not be able to identify the ten horns (kings) specifically, we do see that they are a part of the Roman Empire, and it was this "little horn" that made war with the saints (Daniel 7:24). We also see that this king "speak[s] great words against the most High, and shall wear out the saints… and think to change times and laws: and they shall be given into his hand until a time and times and the dividing of time" (Daniel 7:25).

It is generally accepted that the term "time and times and the dividing of time" is referring to three and one-half years. This is a time frame that carries more than just a measurement of a length of time. Later in the *Book of Daniel*, when speaking of the time of the Messiah, it tells us that "he shall confirm the covenant with many for one week: and in the midst of the week he shall cause the sacrifice and the oblation to cease" (Daniel 9:27). This may sound confusing, but let's break it down, step by step.

Daniel was prophesying of the time when the Messiah will come, and he gives us very specific dates. If we look at the ninth chapter of the *Book of Daniel*, we see that there would be 483 years from the time the commandment was given to rebuild the city of Jerusalem, until the Messiah.

We do know that when Nehemiah and Ezra returned from the Babylonian captivity to rebuild the city and wall of Jerusalem, and according to our calendar, that it would have been 458 B.C. So, according to Daniel, there would be sixty-nine weeks, or 483 years from the time the command was given to rebuild the city, to the Messiah (anointed one).

Let's do a little math. 483-458 B.C. =A.D. 25. But because there is no year "0," the year would be A.D. 26. The prophetic word through Daniel was "after the command to rebuild Jerusalem to the Messiah," so this was not in reference to the birth of Jesus, but when He became the Messiah, that is "The Anointed One." When was Jesus anointed? According to Luke, it was when Jesus turned "about" thirty years of age (Luke 3:22-23).

Keep in mind that our calendar is off by five years. The calendars of Jesus' day measured years from the beginning of the city of Rome. But in the sixth century, the Pope commissioned a monk named Dionysius Exiguus to produce a new calendar; measuring the years from the birth of Jesus. Dionysius erred by estimating the Roman year of Jesus' birth to be 754 *Anno Urbis Conditae* (A.U.C. or year of the founding of the city). Therefore, he made that year, year 1.

It is evident that Jesus was not born in 754, because Herod the Great died in 750. Jesus had to be born prior to King Herod's death, because it was Herod who met the Magi and directed them to Bethlehem to find the newborn Jesus. This same Herod had all the male babies under two years of age killed, in his attempt to kill the newborn King of Israel (Matthew 2:1-16). We know that King Herod died on March 13, 4 B.C., according to our calendar, so Jesus was born prior to 4 B.C.

We may not know the exact date of Jesus' birth; but since He was the fulfillment of all of the seven feasts of Israel, it is worth looking at the previous feast day prior to Herod's death in 4 B.C. That would have been the Feast of Tabernacles, near the end of the month of September.

The Feast of Tabernacles or "Booths," has its origin in Moses' day. God instructed him to command the Israelites, who were wandering in the wilderness, to remember this time once they entered the Promised Land. They would do this by making booths outside of their homes on the fifteenth day of the seventh month.

For seven days, they would celebrate this feast by remembering how God "tabernacled" with them, by dwelling in these booths, in the same way they had lived in tents in the wilderness (Leviticus 23:39-44).

How appropriate it would be for Jesus to be born during this feast? He is the fulfillment of the prophetic word spoken by Isaiah, "Behold, a virgin shall be with child, and shall bring forth a son, and they shall call his name Emmanuel, which being interpreted is, God with us" (see Matthew 1:21-23).

So, if Jesus was born in September in 5 B.C., He would turn thirty years of age in A.D. 26, when he was baptized by John the Baptist and anointed to be the Messiah (Luke 3:21-22).

The prophecy in *Daniel* continues with, "And he shall confirm the covenant with many for one week: and in the midst of the week he shall cause the sacrifice and the oblation to cease..." (Daniel 9:27). So, the Messiah shows up after 483 years, and has come to confirm the covenant for one week (or seven years); but after three and one-half years (the middle of the week), He shall cause the sacrifices to cease.

Jesus is called the "messenger of the covenant" (Malachi 3:1). He had come as the Savior of the world, but He had also come to fulfill the covenant God made with Abraham and his seed. We saw in *Daniel*, that there were 490 years determined for the nation of Israel. When Jesus the Messiah arrived after 483 years, He was to confirm the covenant with Israel for seven years. But after three and one-half years, He would cause the sacrifice to cease.

What happened three and one-half years after Jesus was anointed as Messiah during His baptism by John? He was crucified and the veil of the Temple was torn in two, from the top to the bottom (Matthew 27:51). *There would never be another sacrifice that God would recognize.*

Jesus' redemptive work on the cross as the Lamb of God would, "...finish the transgression, and to make an end of sins, and to make reconciliation for iniquity, and to bring in everlasting righteousness...and he [would] cause the sacrifice and oblation to cease..." (Daniel 9:24,27). All these things were fulfilled by Jesus; even the time frames of seven years and three and one-half years reveal these things.

Seven is a number that, beyond its numerical value, represents perfection, maturity, or completeness. Three and one-half represents a broken covenant; displayed by the chief priests, scribes, Pharisees, and religious leaders of Israel, who rejected Jesus and would not recognize Him as their Messiah. Once again, Israel had broken the covenant with God, as had happened many times throughout their history (Isaiah 24:5; Jeremiah 11:10).

The result of this broken covenant would be the desolation that would come upon the city and people of Jerusalem (Daniel 9:27; Matthew 23:36). Jesus was thirty years old in A.D. 26 when He was anointed as the Messiah. For three and one-half years, He preached the gospel of the kingdom of God and performed countless miracles that bore witness that He was the Christ (Messiah).

He was then crucified and resurrected in A.D. 30, giving Israel forty years to repent; but just as had occurred many times before, because of the rebellion of the people, that generation (forty years) would not pass away until everything Jesus declared against the Temple and the city of Jerusalem would be fulfilled. It was in A.D. 70, that the Roman armies besieged the city of Jerusalem; destroying it and the Temple in the most horrendous destruction of all time.

Now, back to the "little horn" we read about in *Daniel*. In the seventh chapter of *Daniel*, there is a contrasting of events taking place on the earth and in heaven. In the earth, we see the four kingdoms; ending with the Roman Empire, and ten horns or authorities that represent ten kings of Rome. Among these kings, there arose another king who was identified as a "little horn," with eyes and a mouth (Daniel 7:3-8).

The next several verses give us a glimpse of what is happening in heaven. "I kept looking Until thrones were set up, And the Ancient of Days (God) took His seat…The court was seated, And the books were opened" (Daniel 7:9-10 AMP). The result of the boastful words of the little horn were the destruction of the beast and the stripping of authority held by the other beasts (Daniel 7:11-12).

These "beasts" or kingdoms of the world would no longer function by man's highjacked authority that Adam forfeited (Luke 4:6). Instead, all authority and dominion would be given to the Son of God, as Jesus is enthroned with all authority; and "all people, nations, and languages, should serve him" in His eternal kingdom (Matthew 28:18; Daniel 7:13-14).

As Daniel inquired of the Lord about the meaning of this vision, it was explained that, "The four beasts are four earthly kingdoms. But God Most High will give his kingdom to his chosen ones, and it will be theirs forever and ever" (Daniel 7:17-18 CEV). Then Daniel wanted to know about the fourth beast and the horn that exalted itself above all the others, and that made war with the saints for three and one-half years (time, times, and dividing of time).

There are many indications that this "little horn" is in reference to Caesar Nero, who ruled Rome from A.D. 54 to A.D. 68. During his horrific reign, several major events took place. First,

What About the Mark of the Beast?

Rome burned, and many blamed Nero for starting the fire. There never was absolute proof one way or another that he started the fire either by accident or purposefully, but one thing was certain. The Roman people blamed him.

Nero shifted blame to the church by accusing Christians of starting the blaze, in an attempt to turn the people of Rome against the Christians. His systematic attack on the church began with the rounding up of all of the Christian leaders. It was during this time that both the Apostles Paul and Peter were executed, as well as many others. This persecution against the saints began at the end of the year that Rome burned (A.D. 64); and concluded with the death of Nero (June A.D. 68) – a period of three and one-half years.

This chapter began with a question: "What about the mark of the beast?" We have identified the beast or the kingdom, to be Rome, in the time of the Messiah. The government of Rome had evolved by the time Jesus was born. Rome had been governed by Senators, who represented the different provinces of the empire. But by the time of Jesus' birth, Rome was not only controlled by the Senate, but also by an emperor.

One of Rome's most outstanding generals was Julius Caesar. His popularity concerned some of the Senators; they were afraid that he might be made "ruler" and weaken the authority of the Senate. This resulted in Julius Caesar's assassination and the eventual warring between the Roman generals and their armies. The outcome of these battles made General Octavian the victor. Bringing his armies into Rome; he became known as Augustus Caesar.

According to Flavius Josephus (A.D. 37-100, *Antiquities*, books 18, 19); Julius Caesar was the first of the Roman Emperors. He was followed by Augustus, Tiberius, Caligula, Claudius, and the sixth emperor, Nero. As we have already seen, it was Nero who brought three and one-half years of imperial persecution against the Church. According to the *Aramaic Revelation* (in the *Crawford Codex*), the last book of the Bible is titled as, "The Revelation which came to John the Evangelist from God in Patmos the island to which he was exiled by Nero Caesar."

Not only was Nero the Emperor of the Roman Empire, the fourth "beast" that Daniel speaks of; but Nero himself was referred to as "the beast." Just a casual reading of some of the Roman and Jewish historians such as Tacitus, Suetonius, Josephus; or even some of the early church fathers, we see Nero referred to as "the beast," for his murderous and perverted ways.

He killed many of his own family, including his wife and mother, and other members of the Roman elite that he felt threatened him. His paranoia and sexual perversions were common knowledge, and his ruthless acts were met with much public disapproval.

Throughout the *Book of Revelation*, we find that the people of God are "sealed" or "marked" in their foreheads with the name of God (Revelation 7:3;14:1). In contrast, those who worship the image of the beast are also sealed or marked in their foreheads or hands (Revelation 13:16-17).

What are these markings? We need to remember that John is writing to first century believers. These "markings" are not social security numbers or computer chips or vaccines, because none of these things existed at the time. John was bringing a revelation to the people he was writing to; not a mystery, so what would being marked in their hand or forehead mean to them?

The first time we see a reference to the forehead in Scripture, is when a curse was placed upon the ground because of Adam's disobedience. He was told he would have to produce food, "…by the sweat of your brow until you return to the ground" (Genesis 3:19 HCSB).

When Moses was receiving instructions from God about the garments for the High Priest, he was told, "And thou shall make a plate of pure gold, and grave upon it, like the engravings of a signet, Holiness To The Lord". And you shall put it "upon the forefront of the mitre…upon Aaron's forehead…" (Exodus 28:36-38).

Then, in the *Book of Deuteronomy*, Moses is admonishing the people concerning the Word of God, that they are to, "Bind them as a sign on your hand and let them be a symbol on your forehead" (Deuteronomy 6:8 HCSB).

In one of the visions of the prophet Ezekiel, he saw a man clothed in linen, with a writer's inkhorn in his hand. The man was told to go throughout the city of Jerusalem and mark upon the foreheads, all those who mourned over the sin of the city. When others were sent to destroy those who lived in the city, they were commanded not to hurt any of those who had the mark (Ezekiel 9:3-6).

So, we see that a man's forehead is marked by either a curse, or a blessing of protection. The mark on the forehead or hand was a mark of ownership: those who belong to God, or those whose loyalty was to Rome or the emperor of Rome (the beast). These markings were not physical, but identified the heart of the people who either carried the image of the beast, or they were made in the "image and likeness of God" (Genesis 1:26).

Although this was not a physical marking in the flesh of the hand or forehead; there was a marking of those who swore allegiance to the emperor. The mark of the beast, referring to Rome or (more specifically) to Nero, was required for everyone to be able to buy or sell.

"And it makes everyone—small and great, rich and poor, free and slave—to receive a mark on his right hand or on his forehead, so that no one can buy or sell unless he has the mark: the beast's name or the number of its name" (Revelation 13:16-17 CSB).

The forehead and the hand can represent a person's thoughts and works. We see the rejection of Jesus by the Jewish leadership, and their loyalty to Caesar, as they demanded the crucifixion of Christ, declaring, "We have no king but Caesar" (John 19:15).

Israel's apostate religious leaders are described in *Revelation* as the great whore who sits upon the beast and has a name written on her forehead, "MYSTERY, BABYLON THE GREAT, THE MOTHER OF HARLOTS AND ABOMINATIONS OF THE EARTH" (Revelation 17:1-5). This description of apostasy is like Isaiah's, "How the faithful city has become a whore, she who was full of justice! Righteousness lodged in her, but now murderers" (Isaiah 1:21 ESV).

This woman, who has sworn her loyalty to the beast of Rome, is murderous. She is drunk with the blood of the saints. She uses Rome to get rid of Jesus (the crucifixion) and brings severe persecution against the saints.

The apostate Jewish leaders who control the Temple and its vast wealth are represented by the city of Jerusalem; already under the curse of destruction pronounced by Jesus upon that generation (Matthew 23:37-38).

Her identification as "Mystery Babylon" is very appropriate, as Babylon has always been identified with idolatry and the persecuting oppressors of God's people. Jerusalem is also referred to as "Sodom and Egypt, where their Lord was crucified" (Revelation 11:8). These names are not identifying the geographical locations of these ancient cities; but their wicked works and rejection of God, and the affliction and persecution of God's people.

Just as ancient Babylon afflicted the people of God, so now first century Jerusalem has become as Babylon destroying God's people. Its connection with Rome to accomplish its purpose is seen by the harlot riding upon the beast that has seven heads and ten horns, just as Daniel described.

The mark or seal in the hand or forehead for people to buy or sell can also be related to the requirements of those involved in the Roman guilds that practiced "Emperor Worship." The guilds were much like the trade unions of our day. Carpenters, tentmakers, stonecutters, tanners, pottery makers, and many other trades were governed by a guild.

Some of the emperors, like Nero, required their subjects to go yearly to the city square, where there would be a statue of the emperor and an eternal flame. Subjects of Rome would be required to sprinkle incense on the flame and declare that "Caesar is lord." Christians refused this worship of the emperor, and would be disqualified from the Roman guilds; resulting in an inability to work (buy or sell).

John mentions the name or the number of the name of the beast as "666." He says, "Here is wisdom. Let him that has understanding count the number of the beast: for it is the number of a man; and his number is Six hundred threescore and six" (Revelation 13:18).

Unlike Western culture, where letters and numbers have different symbols, Greek and Hebrew letters also carry numerical values; thus, the spelling of a name also has a numeric value. While many famous people throughout history have a name that has a numerical value of 666 in the Greek or Hebrew language, only one fits the context of the dating of the *Book of Revelation*.

We have already seen that the coming of the Messiah to accomplish His redemptive work would take place during the fourth kingdom, mentioned by Daniel, which was Rome. Nero Caesar, or Neron Kesar, the Hebrew spelling of his name, has a numerical value of 666.

This is the same one of whom Daniel says, "…shall speak words against the Most High, and shall wear out the saints of the Most High, and shall think to change the times and the law; and they shall be given into his hand for a time, times, and half a time" (Daniel 7:25 ESV).

The coming persecution Jesus warned the churches about was fulfilled by Emperor Nero (666), who proclaimed himself to be God as he brought the first Imperial persecution against the Church; beginning at the end of A.D. 64, until his death in A.D. 68, three and one-half years later, just as Daniel had prophesied.

It was during this season of persecution that many apostles were martyred, including Peter and Paul. The Muratorian Fragment[3] includes a quote from Papius[4] (A.D. 130) that, "John the Apostle was martyred before the destruction of Jerusalem," which was in A.D. 70.

The two major world events after Jesus' resurrection from the dead would be the persecution of the Church (resulting in the death of the apostles); and the Jewish war against Rome, that ended with the destruction of both the Temple and the city of Jerusalem.

---

[3] The Moratorian Fragment, from the second century, is the oldest listing of New Testament books.

[4] Papius was an early, second century Greek Apostolic Father and the Bishop of Hieropolis.

Chapter 6

Major World Events Following Jesus' Resurrection

Warning of Persecution
Jews Declare War Against Rome

Jesus warned the Jewish religious leaders about the judgment that would come upon them, for the persecution they would bring against those whom Jesus would send to them.

> Woe unto you, scribes and Pharisees, hypocrites!...behold, I send unto you prophets, and wise men, and scribes: and some of them [you] shall kill and crucify; and some of them shall [you] scourge in your synagogues, and persecute them from city to city (Matthew 23:29,34).

Jesus also warned His disciples of the coming persecution they would face. "Then shall they deliver you up to be afflicted, and shall kill you: and [you] shall be hated of all nations for my name's sake" (Matthew 24:9).

The warning of persecution against the Church was a theme often repeated throughout all the New Testament writings. Jesus told Peter (after he had denied Jesus three times) that he would one day lay down his life as a martyr and be crucified (John 21:18-19).

The *Book of Acts* is replete with examples of the persecution brought against Peter and John (Acts chapters 3-5). Stephen was stoned to death (Acts 7). Saul was arresting, beating, and imprisoning believers (Acts 8:1-3). King Herod killed James, the brother of John, with the sword, and arrested Peter; planning on executing him the next day (Acts 12:1-4).

Beginning with chapter 13 of *Acts* and until the end of the book, are records of repeated persecutions against Paul and his ministry team. Paul gives the Corinthian Church a quick history of the things he personally suffered:

> …in labors more abundant, in stripes above measure, in prisons more frequently, in deaths often. From the Jews five times I received forty *stripes* minus one. Three times I was beaten with rods; once I was stoned; three times I was shipwrecked; a night and a day I have been in the deep; *in* journeys often, *in* perils of waters, *in* perils of robbers, *in* perils of *my own* countrymen, *in* perils of the Gentiles, *in* perils in the city, *in* perils in the wilderness, *in* perils in the sea, *in* perils among false brethren; in weariness and toil, in sleeplessness often, in hunger and thirst, in fastings often, in cold and nakedness—besides the other things, what comes upon me daily: my deep concern for all the churches. (2 Corinthians 11:23-28 NKJV).

It was the Jewish religious leaders that constantly brought persecution against Jesus. After His death and resurrection, the persecution from the Jews continued against the Church. In the beginning, it was the Jewish religious leaders who solicited the help of the Roman government, to destroy Jesus, and then the Church.

Pilate and Herod were both involved in the trial of Jesus. Herod Antipas arrested and executed James, the brother of John, because "it pleased the Jews" (Acts 12:3). It wasn't until the days of Roman Emperor Nero that the persecution against the church would become empire-wide. We have already looked at his three and one-half years of intense persecution.

In the previous chapter, we looked at the harlot (apostate Israel), who shed the blood of the people of God; she was riding on the back of the beast with seven heads and ten horns (Roman Empire). With its capital city and Temple in Jerusalem, Israel was in league with Rome to destroy the Church. How then, will this alliance between Rome and Israel be broken – one that would result in the devastation of the city of Jerusalem, the Temple, and the cities Jesus mentioned (Matthew 11:21-24)?

There had long been tension between certain Roman leaders and the Jews. As Rome acquired greater and greater influence in Judea; Roman leaders and laws conflicted with different Jewish factions. The Sadducees and chief rulers who controlled the vast wealth of the Temple in Jerusalem often sought favors from the Roman leaders. And because the Jews were so numerous; many concessions were made to accommodate them.

On the other hand, the Zealots were at odds with both the Jewish leaders and the Roman rulers. These Jewish rebels would enlist militants to bring random attacks against Roman military forces, and Roman and Jewish aristocrats they considered to be in opposition to Judean independence.

Josephus gives a rather detailed listing of these not uncommon conflicts, but it was the violence that began in Caesarea in

A.D. 66, that initiated the three and one-half year conflict that would bring about the destruction of the city of Jerusalem and the Temple.

Certain Greeks began sacrificing birds in front of a synagogue in the city of Caesarea. As a result, the Jewish leaders in Jerusalem stopped the customary prayers and sacrifices for the Roman Emperor. In retaliation, Gessius Florus, the Roman Procurator of Judea, sent Roman troops to the Temple in Jerusalem, and removed seventeen talents from the Temple treasury.

Josephus implies that Florus, who loved money, was willingly provoking a war with the Jews to acquire the wealth contained in the Temple. The Jewish population began publicly mocking Florus, who responded by sending troops to arrest many of the city leaders; having them beaten and crucified. Jewish militant groups quickly took up arms against the Romans in Jerusalem, and seized the Roman garrison there, killing many.

The city of Jerusalem was divided between the rebels, who would not be satisfied with anything less than total independence from Rome, and those who opposed the rebellion and desired to make concessions with the Romans. The conflict between the opposing factions within the city resulted in many being killed, including Ananias, the former high priest.

The hatred between the Jews and the Romans was compounded when the rebels overwhelmed the garrison in Jerusalem. The Roman soldiers surrendered on the condition they would be allowed safe passage out of the city. The rebels agreed, but once the surrender took place, the rebels killed the soldiers.

The Jews had just spit in the eye of the most powerful military force in the world, and would soon reap the consequences. It was also during this time that the Sicarii rebels invaded the Roman garrison at Masada, and seized control of the fortress there. It was now plain to the Roman Emperor that the Jewish rebellion had to be quickly crushed.

It seemed that the level of conflict escalated quickly, as there had been a long struggle between the Jews and the Greeks in many cities. In Alexandria, a conflict arose that brought destruction to all the Jewish quarters in that city; resulting in the deaths of fifty thousand Jews, including men, women, infants, and the aged, who all lay in heaps around the city. With each uprising, the hatred between the Jews and the Romans intensified.

Roman Emperor Nero sent Cestius from Syria to crush the rebellion and restore peace. Cestius took the entire twelfth legion from Antioch and joined with thousands of horsemen, foot soldiers, and archers from other Roman legions; and those from northeast Syria, near the Euphrates River, as well as soldiers from the many auxiliary armies of kings Antiochus, Sohemus, and Agrippa.

It was King Agrippa who went with Cestius to the city of Zabulon. Cestius divided his army; sending some to Joppa and Caesarea, who marched through Galilee, setting on fire and plundering Jewish cities on his way to Jerusalem. (Josephus: *The Wars of the Jews*, book 2; chpt. 18, sect. 9)

Arriving in Jerusalem, Cestius attacked the north side of the Temple with a massive number of large stones from the catapults; driving the Jewish rebels from the wall. Undermining the wall, the Romans were in position to gain complete victory, when Cestius inexplicably withdrew his forces and retreated to Syria.

Some believe his military leaders encouraged him to fall back and revamp his strategy because some of his siege equipment had been destroyed. Rumors that his supply lines could be cut off may have been the cause for his quick retreat. This poor decision prompted the Jews to pursue the Romans, who suffered many casualties during their retreat. This defeat of Cestius emboldened the Jews to believe that God had delivered them from the invading Romans; and prompted the Jews to create a national defense force to oppose Rome.

Cestius died in Syria the following year, and Nero ordered Vespasian to invade Palestine and crush the Jewish revolt. But in the interim, it is recorded that the Christians in Jerusalem fled the city; having been instructed by the words of Jesus, "When you see Jerusalem being surrounded by armies, you will know that its desolation is near. Then let those who are in Judea flee to the mountains, let those in the city get out, and let those in the country not enter the city" (Luke 21:20-21 NIV).

Matthew's account says, "Therefore when you see the 'abomination of desolation,' spoken of by Daniel the prophet, standing in the holy place" (whoever reads, let him understand), "then let those who are in Judea flee to the mountains. Let him who is on the housetop not go down to take anything out of his house. And let him who is in the field not go back to get his clothes… For then there will be great tribulation, such as has not been since the beginning of the world until this time, no, nor ever shall be" (Matthew 24:15-18,21 NKJV).

The fourth century church fathers Eusebius and Epiphanius wrote that Jerusalem's Jewish Christians fled to Pella before the beginning of the war. Other reports say that there were no Christians in the city; for all had fled when they saw the Roman standards – pennants or banners that attached to long poles, to identify the different Roman legions by an image of a serpent, boar, wolf, horse, or eagle (*World History Encyclopedia*).

Vespasian ordered his son Titus to Alexandria, to organize two Roman legions and meet him at Jerusalem. Vespasian took his army from Antioch in Syria and combined it with the auxiliary armies of the kings, to rendezvous at Jerusalem with Titus and his forces.

While the city of Jerusalem was under siege by the Romans outside the walls; inside were three major factions of rebels fighting each other. The priests and Temple rulers who were cloistered in the Holy Place would have welcomed the Romans, had they gained the opportunity, but they were constantly in fear for their lives and were being threatened by the rebel factions.

The rebels led by Eleazar and his party were at war with John and his army; and Simon and his party made war against the others. Each of these had a considerable force with them. Eleazar commanded more than ten thousand men, and John's army exceeded six thousand. Their constant fighting led to the fire that burned all the houses of grain that had been stored up to supply the city in case of a siege.

The destruction of grain that could have fed the people for several years now hastened the condition of starvation within the walls of the city. Soon, no mercy was shown to anyone who had food. Men, women, and children all perished who were found with any provision; people even snatched food out of the mouths of the feeblest, even as they were run through by the swords of the desperate.

Having destroyed some of the cities surrounding Jerusalem, and placing garrisons in strategic locations, Vespasian returned to Caesarea. He was preparing his vast army to march on Jerusalem when he received news of Nero's death. Almost immediately, Rome was entangled in a civil war. Roman generals rallied around leaders and declared their favorites as the new emperor.

Factions fought in the streets of Rome as the city fell into great distress and food supplies became scarce. Galba, Otho, and Vitellius were all hailed as emperor, but all were slain by their rivals within months of each other. Vespasian ordered his son Titus to siege Jerusalem while he and his armies went to Egypt to secure the necessary supplies of grain for Rome. He was declared emperor by his military leaders. Then he returned to Rome, where he took charge of the government, restored peace, and supplied much-needed provisions to the people.

Meanwhile, in Jerusalem, Titus assembled the catapults and sent a hailstorm of stones weighing nearly a talent each (60 pounds) against the walls of the city. Josephus describes the cry of those on the walls, who attempted to warn those in the city where the stones would land. "The Son Cometh" is the English translation of Josephus' record of the warning of those on the wall. The catapult stones were white in color, but the Romans painted them black to make their flight path harder to see (Josephus: *The Wars of the Jews*, book 5; chpt. 6; sect. 3).

The utter destruction of the city of Jerusalem, the Temple, and the atrocities within and without the city are described in detail by many historians. Josephus, Tacitus, Suetonius, and others reveal how the lands around the city of Jerusalem were deforested to supply the thousands of crosses used to crucify those who escaped the city.

Starvation within the city caused many to try and flee in the night. News that those deserting the city had swallowed their gold caused them to be disemboweled upon capture. Those remaining within the city suffered the most horrendous brutality. In the end, the city and Temple were destroyed, where "not one stone was left upon another" (Matthew 24:2).

Major World Events Following Jesus' Resurrection

The words of Jesus were perfectly fulfilled when He answered His disciples' questions about "when shall these things be" (Matthew 24:3)? Jesus said, "Verily I say unto you, This generation shall not pass, till all these things be fulfilled" (Matthew 24:34). Jesus was crucified, resurrected, and ascended into heaven, just days after He had declared these things. Forty years later (one generation), the city of Jerusalem and the Temple were both destroyed, just as He had declared they would be.

Chapter 7

The Book of Revelation

INTRODUCTION – SEVEN CHURCHES

When was the *Book of Revelation* written? It is of uttermost importance that we determine the time frame of the writing of this book by the Apostle John. The significance of the date is directly related to the events described in the book, because in both the introduction to the *Book of Revelation* and in the conclusion, references are made to things that were about to happen. "…things which must shortly come to pass…for the time is at hand…Seal not the sayings of the prophecy of this book: for the time is at hand" (Revelation 1:1,3; 22:10).

I have read many commentaries that date the writing of *Revelation* to be around A.D. 96, during the reign of the Roman Emperor Domitian. There is really no verifiable evidence to support this late date. If *Revelation* was written during this time, then what events took place shortly after its writing that could have been related to the events described in the chapters of this book? There are none.

But if *Revelation* was written around A.D. 60; then many of the persecutions, tribulations, and judgments described in the book can be related to the historical accounts we have from first century historians, who were eyewitnesses of these things taking place between A.D. 64 and A.D. 70.

There are also extant writings of the Syriac version of the New Testament, dating from the second century A.D., which state that *Revelation* was written during the reign of Nero, who we remember was emperor from A.D. 54 to A.D. 68.

Also, the Muratorian Fragment that dates to 170 to 190 A.D., contains a quote from Papias (A.D. 130), stating that John the Apostle was martyred before the destruction of Jerusalem (A.D. 70). I have already mentioned that according to the Aramaic Revelation (in the *Crawford Codex*), the last book of the Bible is titled as, "The Revelation which came to John the Evangelist from God in Patmos the island to which he was exiled by Nero Caesar."

The messages given to the churches are all about preparation, correction, and warning, regarding events that were about to take place. Difficult years beginning in A.D. 64 to A.D. 70 lay ahead of them. Imperial persecution against the Church began in late A.D. 64 and lasted until Nero's death in A.D. 68 (again, a time frame of three and one-half years).

In A.D. 66, the Jewish war against Rome began under Nero's reign but concluded in A.D. 70 (another three and one-half years), when the city of Jerusalem and the Temple were burned to the ground. The horrific events described in *Revelation* correspond to the three and one-half years, forty-two months; and 1,260 day time frames mentioned throughout the last book of the Bible.

The *Book of Revelation* begins with, "The Revelation of Jesus Christ, which God gave unto him, to [show] unto his servants things which must shortly come to pass; and he sent and signified it by his angel unto his servant John" (Revelation 1:1). This revelation to John was to be given to the seven churches of Asia Minor, who were listed by name – and the essence of this revelation was to be communicated to them in signs and symbols (signified).

There is no question that this book contains many symbols that these churches would understand. This is a "revelation" given, not a mystery. Many of the symbols are numbers, animals, furnishings, and other things that the Christian community of believers would understand. John is describing to the churches, all the things that he saw. It is noteworthy that John first "hears" something and then turns to "see" the fulfillment of what he had just heard (Revelation 1:12).

The Lord Jesus Christ is described as clothed with a long garment that extended to His feet, with a golden belt; and having extremely white hair and eyes like a flame of fire. And from His mouth came a two-edged sword. He stood in the middle of a seven-branched lampstand, with seven stars in His right hand. His countenance was as bright as the sun (Revelation 1:13-16 NKJV).

Immediately, we see symbols that John explains. The seven stars are the angels (messengers) to the churches, and the seven-branched lampstand represents the seven churches (Revelation 1:20). Some of the other symbols are not explained here, but are seen in other Scriptures. The sharp two-edged sword coming out of the mouth of Jesus is found in *Hebrews 4:12*, which describes the Word of God as living and powerful, and sharper than any two-edged sword. The sword that is coming out of His mouth is obviously the Word of God.

We see Jesus standing in the "midst" of the seven-branched lampstand. Two things come to mind with this image. The first is the holy place within Moses' tabernacle, and then later, the

Temple, which contained the seven-branched lampstand, the table of showbread, and the golden altar of incense.

There were no windows in that place, so the only light was produced by the oil lamps that were held by the seven-branched lampstand. Jesus said that we are the light of the world (Matthew 5:14). Therefore, the churches that are represented by the seven-branched lampstand hold the light.

Secondly, Jesus said that He is the vine and we are the branches (John 15:5). This lampstand has seven branches; each is attached to Jesus, as He stands as the one who holds the stars (angels or messengers) to these seven churches. The necessity for the branches (churches) to be attached to Jesus (the vine, centerpiece of the seven-branched lampstand) is so that they will bear fruit that can only come by the nourishment the vine provides.

In the Temple, the menorah was made of solid gold. It had seven branches that were attached to a centerpiece that resembled the trunk of a tree. On top of the seven branches were seven golden lamps (containers of oil which fed a wick that burned to give light and expose the fruit that was engraved upon the branches) (Exodus 25:31-40).

Most of the symbols in this first chapter of *Revelation* are not difficult to understand. The fruit of the Spirit is borne upon the branches (churches) that are fed by the vine (Jesus) and which hold the light (revelation) to the world.

In chapters two and three, there are descriptions of the seven churches that Jesus told John to address in chapter one. Although these were actual churches in Asia Minor (Turkey today), they were also representative of all of the churches.

The number seven is used extensively throughout this book. There are seven churches, seven angels, seven thunders, seven

Spirits of God, seven lampstands, seven seals, seven horns, seven eyes, seven trumpets, and the list goes on. "Seven" in Scripture represents completion, perfection, and wholeness. Although these were actual seven churches that had distinctive characteristics, strengths, and weaknesses; they were indicative of all of the churches; not just those in Asia Minor.

As Jesus addresses certain needs that characterize these individual churches, those same concerns could be warnings and instructions to all of the churches of that day, as well as those throughout all ages. For example, the Church in Ephesus had many good works, but Jesus had an indictment against them because they had "left their first love" (Revelation 2:4). They were admonished to repent and do the first (best) works or their church (lampstand) would be moved "out of his place" (Revelation 2:5).

In this rebuke, two things come to mind. The first was when Jesus was at Martha's house with His disciples. As He was teaching, Mary, Martha's sister, sat listening at His feet. Martha was busy preparing a meal, and resented the fact that Mary was not helping her. Martha appealed to Jesus to make Mary help her, but Jesus replied that Martha was careful and troubled about many things, but Mary had chosen the "good" part (Luke 10:41-42).

The Church at Ephesus was busy and working hard, but the people had forsaken their first or best love. A lesson for all churches is that works are good, but they are only profitable if done out of love for Jesus.

The appropriate response for this church was to "repent" (from a Greek word meaning "with thought" or "to think differently, i.e., change the mind"). The Church at Ephesus needed to think differently about what they were doing, and why. They were busy in the kitchen but had abandoned their most important place at the feet of Jesus.

The warning of being moved "out of place" was a phrase well-known to those who lived in the city of Ephesus; which was a port city on the Aegean Sea. The Cayster River emptied into the port, and the silt from the river filled the port; which required constant dredging to keep the port operational. Failure to dredge the mud and silt out of the harbor would result in the water level becoming too shallow for the ships to enter. There was a real threat for this city to maintain its position and not be cut off from the sea. A major engineering project had dredged the port many years earlier; but over time, the harbor was being endangered. In the middle of the first century, the harbor was again dredged, and the port was maintained.

Today, after centuries of neglect, the ancient city of Ephesus is six miles from the coast. In like manner, the church at Ephesus was in danger of losing its strategic position of influence. The lampstand needed to be vitally attached to Jesus so it could bear the light (revelation) it was meant to exhibit.

The Church in Smyrna was warned about the soon-coming persecution, "Behold, the devil is about to throw some of you into prison, that you may be tested, and for ten days you will have tribulation. Be faithful unto death, and I will give you a crown of life" (Revelation 2:10 ESV).

The city of Pergamos is described as being "where Satan's throne is" (Revelation 2:13 NIV). Robert H. Mounce states, "Frequent mention is made of the great throne-like altar to Zeus, which overlooked the city from the citadel" (*The Book of Revelation*. Grand Rapids: William B. Eerdmans Publishing Co., 1977, page 96f). Also in the city, was the cult of Asklepios, who was designated as "Savior," and whose symbol was the serpent.

Pergamos was also the center for Emperor Worship in the East. Allegiance to Rome was prominent. Jesus praised the faithful there, who were under great persecution, but He also warned those who held the doctrine of Balaam and the Nicolaitans. Balaam, the prophet from Mesopotamia, whose name in Hebrew means "foreigner" or "lord of the people," attempted to curse the people of God for rewards promised him from Balak, the king of the Moabites, and an enemy of Israel.

An angel with a drawn sword was prepared to kill Balaam for his conspiracy against God. Later, he did die by the sword of the armies of Israel, but he first taught the enemies of Israel how to seduce them and rob them of victories.

The name "Nicolaitans" has a similar meaning in Greek: "conqueror of the people." These cults were designed to seduce the people of God. No wonder Jesus said that He would come and fight against them with the "sword of my mouth" (Revelation 2:16).

The Church in the city of Thyatira faced many challenges. The city was governed by trade guilds and was a center of Emperor Worship. Workers were obligated to be a member of one of the many guilds, and worship the pagan deity that governed that guild. The pagan deities required members to eat meat that was sacrificed to that deity, and to participate in illicit sexual activities.

The primary pagan god over Thyatira was "Tyrimnos," who was identified as the "son of Zeus." Caesar was also worshiped and proclaimed to be the "Son of God." No wonder Jesus identifies Himself as the "Son of God, who [has] his eyes like unto a flame of fire, and his feet are like fine brass" (Revelation 2:18).

Jesus praised the faithful in the Church at Thyatira, but condemned those leaders in the church, who allowed that spirit of Jezebel to seduce His servants to commit fornication and to eat meat sacrificed to idols.

Jezebel was well-known as the wicked wife of Ahab, who was the king of Israel in the ninth century B.C. She was a worshiper of "Baal," and actively promoted Baal worship throughout the nation. It was the 450 prophets of Baal that Jezebel provided for, during a time of great famine, that the prophet Elijah destroyed on Mount Carmel.

Just as Jezebel greatly influenced her husband the king, and led all the nation of Israel into the worship of the false god Baal; so the wicked spirit that ruled over the city of Thyatira had influenced some in the church to participate in these pagan practices.

The Church at Sardis was encouraged to "wake up" and "watch" because it was "dead" (lifeless, inactive, void of power, destitute of life). The life of Christ was to be exemplified through the Church, to reach the city, but the Lord said, "I have not found your works perfect (complete) before God" (Revelation 3:2). There was no correction brought to this church because of false teaching or Emperor Worship; or even a mention of persecution.

The problem was a lack of influence or fruitfulness, to transform the city. It was dead, for all practical purposes. And because it was not "watching" (perceiving) what was happening spiritually, it would be caught by surprise when both the coming persecution from Rome and judgment pronounced upon that generation would be fulfilled. Jesus' coming to them would be "like a thief" – by surprise and wholly unexpected.

Believers whose names are written in the Lamb's book of life were not to continue to wear the filthy garments of the "old man," but were to walk before those of the city in righteous garments; demonstrating the kingdom of God and the love of Jesus by putting on the garments of the "new man" (Ephesians 4:24).

The Church in Philadelphia is told that Jesus knows their works and that He sees that they have kept His Word and have not denied (contradicted) His name, although they only had a "little strength." To them, there was an open door that no man could shut.

The imagery here reminds us of *Isaiah 22*, where the Lord sees the wicked works of Shebna, who is the treasurer for the Temple of God. The Lord says that He will remove him and give His glory, strength, and authority to another: Eliakim (whose name means "God raises," or "God sets up"), who is faithful.

This "faithful one" has the authority of the government upon his shoulder and is given the key to the house of David, to open or shut doors as he wills (Isaiah 22:15-22). This reminds us of Jesus, who has the eternal and ever-increasing government of God upon His shoulder (Isaiah 9:6-7); and He has the keys of hell and death (Revelation 1:18).

Unlike the Church at Sardis that was sleeping on the job, the Philadelphian Church had works that did not contradict the name of Jesus. Just like John who saw an "open door" in heaven (Revelation 4:1), the Philadelphian Church had an open door before them, and their faithfulness gave them authority to access the things in the heavenly realm.

The unfaithful Jews, who were supposed to represent the people of God, are instead, the synagogue of Satan that persecutes the true believers who have access to the city of God (New Jerusalem) and the name of God that they carry. The pillars in the Temple at Jerusalem will soon be thrown down, but the people of God are the pillars of the true Temple.

One promise to the Church at Philadelphia is that Jesus will keep them from the "hour of temptation," which shall come upon all the land. If this great tribulation was not going to take place for several thousand years in their future, then this promise would be meaningless. But the time is near and the message to the churches reveals the things they will soon experience.

The last of the seven churches is Laodicea (meaning: "righteousness of the people"). To the Laodiceans, the Lord identifies Himself as the "Amen," the "Faithful and True Witness," and the "Beginning of the Creation of God" (Revelation 3:14). Jesus, identifying Himself with these titles, stands in contrast to the qualities of this church. As the "Amen," Jesus is the "absolute reliable certainty" of the covenant. He is the one who bears witness to the truth, for He is the creator and originator of all things.

The Church at Laodicea has the *appearance* of righteousness, success, and wealth, but it is really only self-righteous, blind, and naked. Jesus uses this church's reputation, geographical location, and primary industries to characterize how He sees them.

The city of Laodicea is nestled in a valley south of the city of Hierapolis, and west of the city of Colossae. Each of these cities is distinguished by its natural resources. Hierapolis was known for its hot mineral springs, and Colossae for its cold, pure water. Both unique resources were beneficial to the people.

Traveling from all over the region, people would go to soak in the hot mineral springs for their physical health. Colossae provided cold, pure water from the melting snow from the nearby mountains. This water was carried by aqueducts to neighboring regions.

However, Laodicea's water was the result of the hot, mineralized water from Hierapolis that ran down the cliffs and into the valley. By the time it reached Laodicea, it was only "lukewarm," and the taste of sulfur made it undrinkable. The Church at Laodicea had works that were like its useless water: "neither hot nor cold."

The city of Laodicea was renowned for its three major industries. It was a wealthy city because of its banking center and gold exchange. They also produced fine black glossy wool that was used to make expensive garments. And its medical school was known throughout Asia Minor for its eyesalve, known as Phrygian powder, which had been produced there since the days of Aristotle.

Jesus addresses the self-righteous church as those who say, "I am rich, and increased with goods, and have need of nothing;" they can't see they are "wretched, and miserable, and poor, and blind, and naked" (Revelation 3:17). The counsel Jesus gave to this church was to come to Him and buy "gold" (that which has true value); and to cover their nakedness with the white robes of righteousness and anoint their eyes with eye salve so they could see clearly (Revelation 3:18).

This compromising church was of little use for the kingdom of God. There was no mention of persecution at Laodicea, because they had conformed to the world around them, instead of being the transforming factor that would bring the city to Christ. Jesus invites this church to open the door to Him and He would come to them. And in that place of fellowship, He would counsel them about how to resolve their failures and reign in life as overcomers.

Chapter 8

John's Vision of Heaven

ACTIVATION OF THE NEW TESTAMENT
OPENING THE SEALS AND THE COMPLETION
OF THE OLD TESTAMENT

IN CHAPTER ONE OF *REVELATION*, we read of John's testimony regarding his exile, and the vision of Jesus he received while on the isle of Patmos. The description of Jesus prepared the tone of the messages to the seven churches to whom John was to write.

Chapters two and three are the messages to the churches, that warn them of soon-coming persecution; and areas of correction that some needed to make, in order to overcome the rising tide of adversity and heresy.

Chapters four and five concern John's vision of events taking place in heaven, and explain what is about to take place on earth. In this vision, John is caught up into heaven, where he sees the throne of God. Encircling the throne, are twenty-four thrones; and on those thrones are twenty-four elders, who have golden crowns. It is not difficult to determine who these ruling elders are, considering the following Scriptures:

"To him that [overcomes], will I grant to sit with me in my throne, even as I also overcame, and am set down with my Father in his throne" (Revelation 3:21).

"…[you] which have followed me, in the regeneration when the Son of man shall sit in the throne of his glory, [you] also shall sit upon twelve thrones, judging the twelve tribes of Israel" (Matthew 19:28).

"And [has] raised us up together, and made us sit together in heavenly places in Christ Jesus" (Ephesians 2:6).

"And has made us unto our God kings and priests: and we shall reign on the earth" (Revelation 5:10).

"And I heard the number of them which were sealed…an hundred and forty-four thousand of all the tribes of the children of Israel" (Revelation 7:4).

"And had a wall…and had twelve gates…and names written thereon, which are the names of the twelve tribes of the children of Israel" (Revelation 21:12).

"And the wall of the city had twelve foundations, and in them the names of the twelve apostles of the Lamb" (Revelation 21:14).

"And the city [lies] foursquare, and the length is as large as the breadth: and he measured the city with the reed, twelve thousand furlongs. The length and the breadth and the height of it are equal. And he measured the wall thereof, a hundred and forty and four cubits…" (Revelation 21:16-17).

These few Scriptures show us the meaning of the number twelve, that we have discussed in previous chapters. Twelve is the number associated with the government, or the people of God.

John's Vision of Heaven

The twelve tribes of Israel are represented by twelve of the twenty-four elders about the throne. The twelve apostles are represented by the other twelve. Together, they represent all of the saints in both the Old and New Testaments.

John was summoned by one of the angels, who showed him the "bride," who was the Lamb's wife, or the Bride of Christ (Revelation 21:9). John saw the "holy city, New Jerusalem, coming down from God ... prepared as a bride adorned for her husband" (Revelation 21:2).

When the angel showed him the bride (Church), it was a city with the names of the twelve tribes of Israel on its twelve gates. And it had twelve foundations with the names of the twelve Apostles of the Lamb.

Again, this city is described as a cube or foursquare; with its length, breadth, and height each twelve-thousand furlongs. John also heard the number of the servants of God, who were sealed in their foreheads. The number of them was an hundred and forty-four thousand (12,000 x 12). But when he turned to see them, they were a "great multitude, which no man could number, of all nations, and kindreds, and people, and tongues..." (Revelation 7:3-4,9).

So, these twenty-four elders encircling the throne of God are representative of all believers. The beauty of the throne room is shown to John. He sees the sea of glass, the seven lamps of fire, the seven Spirits of God, and the four "living creatures," like the seraphim that Isaiah and Ezekiel had seen about the throne (Isaiah 6:1-3; Ezekiel 1:5-11).

In chapter five, John's vision continues. He sees a scroll that is sealed with seven seals, and an angel, who asks, "...Who is worthy to break the seals and open the scroll" (Revelation 5:2 NIV)?

According to German Protestant theologian and biblical scholar Theodor Zahn, only a testament was to be sealed with seven seals.

Just prior to Jesus' suffering on the cross for man's redemption; at the "last supper," Jesus said to His disciples, "For this is my blood of the New Testament, which is shed for many for the remission of sins." (Matthew 26:28).

The *Book of Hebrews* tells us that a testament can only be enforced after the death of the testator (Hebrews 9:16). When the angel asked, "Who is worthy to break the seals and open the scroll?" there was no one anywhere found to be qualified. But suddenly, Jesus, the "Lion of the tribe of Judah…has triumphed. He is able to open the scroll and its seven seals" (Revelation 5:1-5 NIV).

When John turned to see the Lion, he sees instead, a Lamb that had been slain in the midst of the throne. It was the slain Lamb who was qualified to take the scroll and open the seals. This resulted in the twenty-four elders (all of the redeemed) and the four seraphim falling down in worship; offering incense (the prayers of the saints) and singing a new song to the Lamb:

> You are worthy to take the scroll,
> And to open its seals;
> For You were slain,
> And have redeemed us to God by Your blood
> Out of every tribe and tongue and people and nation,
> And have made us kings and priests to our God;
> And we shall reign on the earth (Revelation 5:9-10 NKJV).

This Lamb that was slain was the testator of the New Testament. He died to activate the will, and then was resurrected from the dead to administrate His own testament; releasing the inheritance for the saints to be redeemed, and to be made to rule as kings and priests. Contained in the sealed scroll was the will of God that was to be read and conferred upon the saints; and Jesus, the Lamb of God, was the only one who could break its seals and declare its contents.

Chapter six begins with Jesus, the Lamb of God, opening six of the seven seals of the scroll. As the first four seals are opened, we see four horsemen with their respective riders being released in the earth. The four "living creatures," or "beasts" or "seraphim" about the throne give a command to the four horsemen to "come" or "go" (both are translated from the same Greek word), to fulfill their mission in the earth or the land of Israel.

Several translations have the phrase "come and see," which suggests that they were speaking to John, but many translations do not have the word "see," such as the *New International Version*. The seraphim about the throne give directions to the four horsemen to "go" and fulfill their mission. As the horsemen are sent on their way, certain events are accomplished in the earth.

Remember, the *Book of Revelation* is dealing with both the persecution against the Church, and the judgment of Israel's religious leaders; who reject Jesus as Messiah and who stand in opposition to Jesus, who is "building His Church." Jesus declares judgment on Jerusalem, the Temple, and the cities of Galilee in that generation (forty-year time frame from Jesus' resurrection to the destruction of the Temple). And the time was approaching when all of these things would be fulfilled.

The first rider to be released in the earth sits on a white horse, and he goes forth conquering and to conquer, with a bow; wearing a crown. We see this same rider in chapter 19:11-13. This is none other than the Lord Jesus, who is crowned with many crowns, and whose name is the Word of God.

Jesus was coming to fulfill the prophetic Word He gave to the Jewish leaders, when He said to the high priest, "…. [you] shall see the Son of man sitting on the right hand of power, and coming in the clouds of heaven" (Matthew 26:64).

Jesus had already declared to His disciples that He would return in judgment, at the conclusion of that generation, "… all the tribes of the land will mourn, and they shall see the Son of man coming in the clouds of heaven with power and great glory" (Matthew 24:30 PARAPHRASED). This is also described in prophetic language in one of David's psalms:

> Gird your sword on your side, you mighty one;
> clothe yourself with splendor and majesty.
> In your majesty ride forth victoriously
> in the cause of truth, humility, and justice;
> let your right hand achieve awesome deeds.
> Let your sharp arrows pierce the heart of the king's enemies;
> let the nations fall beneath your feet (Psalm 45:3-5 NIV).

Jesus declares eight "woes" of the coming judgment for the cities that had rejected Him (Matthew 11:21-24), and upon the Pharisees, scribes, and hypocrites of that generation (Matthew 23:13-36).

With the breaking of the first seal, the rider of the white horse is coming in the clouds of judgment to fulfill the words of Jesus (Revelation 6:1-2).

The second seal of the scroll was broken by the Lamb, and the second seraphim said to another horse and rider, "Go." This rider was given a great sword, and the people of the land rose to kill one another (Revelation 6:3-4). War broke out throughout all of Israel, as the Roman armies fought against the Jewish militias;

and the Jewish rebels fought against both the Romans and rival Jewish factions.

With the breaking of the third seal, a black horse was sent, whose rider carried a pair of balances; showing that even the most basic food supplies were rationed. A day's labor could only supply a little food (Revelation 6:5-6).

The fourth seal released a green horse, whose rider was death. Everywhere he went, the grave followed. This judgment would kill a fourth of those in the land by sword (war), hunger (famine), death (plagues), and wild beasts (Revelation 6:7-8). These same four judgments of God are seen in Ezekiel.

> So will I send upon you famine and evil beasts, and they shall bereave thee: and pestilence and blood shall pass through thee; and I will bring the sword upon thee. I the LORD have spoken it (Ezekiel 5:17).

> For thus saith the Lord GOD; How much more when I send my four sore judgments upon Jerusalem, the sword, and the famine, and the noisome beasts, and the pestilence, to cut off from it man and beast (Ezekiel 14:21)?

In Ezekiel's day, these judgments upon Jerusalem would be fulfilled by the Babylonians; and in John's day, by the Romans. What would four horses and riders mean to the people of John's day? We need to remember that the New Testament books had not yet been compiled. The Scriptures used by the first century Church were primarily the Old Testament books and some of the letters written by Paul, Peter, John, and the gospel writers.

Would the churches at Ephesus, Philadelphia, or Laodicea have any reference to the first four seals; that when broken, would release these horses and riders to bring judgment upon the land? Yes. In the *Book of Zechariah*, we find a vision the prophet had of four horses and riders (Zechariah 1:8). When the prophet asked, "What are these?" the angel answered, "These [are] they whom Jehovah [has] sent to walk up and down in the land" (Zechariah 1:10 YLT).

Like the command by the four seraphim to "go," these four went throughout the land to report the condition of the nations that had brought such severe judgment upon Jerusalem. Those who had been used of God to destroy the city and the Temple, are represented by four horns (or authorities, usually kings or nations) to scatter "Judah, Israel, and Jerusalem" (Zechariah 1:19).

Again, in chapter six of *Zechariah*, we see four chariots; each pulled by red, black, white, and bay horses, respectively. These are the four "winds" or "spirits" of the heavens that stand before the Lord of all the earth (Zechariah 6:5). This is much like the four "living creatures" or seraphim who surround the throne of God, and who send out the four horsemen to bring judgment upon Jerusalem and the Temple of John's day. These four will summon the Roman armies that will destroy the city of Jerusalem and Temple, with the same four judgments of famine, pestilence, war, and wild beasts.

When the fifth seal was broken, John sees what is happening in heaven; including the souls of those who had been slain on the earth, because of their testimony regarding Jesus and the Word of God.

Jesus had already declared to the religious leaders in the Temple, "…I am sending to you prophets and wise men and teachers. Some of them you will kill and crucify…" (Matthew 23:34 NCV). We know that Stephen was stoned in Jerusalem and James was killed by the sword at Herod's command, because "it pleased the Jews" (Acts 12:1-3). Paul was beheaded in Rome, and Peter was crucified at about the same time (A.D. 67 and 68).

Many church leaders had been arrested at the command of the Emperor Nero, and many had been killed. Now, John sees their souls in heaven, under the altar (the place of sacrifice). Those who had been martyred for their faith were crying out to God with a familiar cry, "How long, Sovereign Lord, holy and true, until you judge the inhabitants of the earth and avenge our blood?" (Revelation 6:10 NIV).

"How long" is a familiar cry to God, asking for His judgment upon the wicked:

"O God, how long shall the adversary reproach? shall the enemy blaspheme thy name for ever" (Psalm 74:10)?

"How long, Lord? wilt thou be angry for ever? shall thy jealousy burn like fire? Pour out thy wrath upon the heathen that have not known thee, and upon the kingdoms that have not called upon thy name" (Psalm 79:5-6).

"Lord, how long shall the wicked, how long shall the wicked triumph? How long shall they utter and speak hard things? and all the workers of iniquity boast themselves" (Psalm 94:3-4)?

Recorded in the pages of the Old Testament are many other times where this cry for God to destroy the wicked was heard. Here, in *Revelation*, we see God's response. White robes were given to every one of these martyrs, and instructions were given to them to rest until the time was fulfilled when others that would also be killed would be accomplished.

Remember, there were three and one-half years of severe persecution that was foreseen by the prophet Daniel. "This king will speak against the Most High God, and he will hurt and kill God's holy people. He will try to change times and laws that have already been set. The holy people that belong to God will be in that king's power for three and one-half years" (Daniel 7:25 NCV).

These martyrs must rest and wait for this Imperial persecution that began at Nero's command at the end of A.D. 64; and lasted until his death on June 9, A.D. 68, which was completed three and one-half years later.

When the sixth seal is opened, John sees what is happening in the earth, because of God's wrath. There is a great earthquake; the sun becomes black, the moon looks like blood, and the stars fall from heaven upon the earth. Heaven departs as a scroll being closed, and the mountains are moved out of their places. These dramatic events cause all people of every social status to hide in caves and dens, and to call upon the mountains and rocks to fall on them, to hide them from this great wrath of the Lamb (Revelation 6:12-17).

We have already discussed the symbolism of a blackened sun and moon; and stars falling from heaven, as described in chapter one of this book. These events are metaphorical, not literal. Quite obviously, if the sun and moon went dark, and the stars fell from heaven, then hiding in caves would not save anyone's life! The sun, moon, and stars are representative of a kingdom. When those things go dark, it means that the kingdom is over. God is turning out the lights over Jerusalem and the land of Israel.

In A.D. 70, the Temple and the city of Jerusalem were completely destroyed. God's judgment was completed, just as Jesus describes in *Matthew 23*. Jesus also described these same events on His way to the cross.

> And a great multitude of the people followed Him, and women who also mourned and lamented Him. But Jesus, turning to them, said, "Daughters of Jerusalem, do not

weep for Me, but weep for yourselves and for your children. For indeed the days are coming in which they will say, 'Blessed *are* the barren'…Then they will begin 'to say to the mountains, "Fall on us!" and to the hills, "Cover us!" 'For if they do these things in the green wood, what will be done in the dry'" (Luke 23:27-31 NKJV)?

Chapter seven is inserted between the opening of the sixth and the seventh seals. Four angels are standing at the four corners of the earth, or the "land" of Israel; holding back the four winds that were about to blow God's judgment over the land. Before this great tribulation could begin (verse 14), the servants of God were to be sealed in their foreheads. We have already looked at the meanings of the seal of God in the hand or the forehead, in chapter five of this book. One who is "sealed" is identified as the possession of the owner; and His property is kept and protected from the "coming wrath."

The wrath of God is against the "beast" Nero, who is an enemy of the Church; and against apostate Israel, who rejected Christ, and who persecutes His Church. God's wrath in judgment against His enemies is not meant for His people. When John the Baptist was preaching in the wilderness, he asked the Pharisees who came to him, "O generation of vipers, who hath warned you to flee from the wrath to come" (Matthew 3:7)?

It would be that same generation who would experience the great tribulation. Paul writing to the Thessalonians encourages them to:

> …wait for his Son from heaven, whom he raised from the dead, even Jesus, which delivered us from the wrath to come" and to know that "…God hath not appointed us to wrath, but to obtain salvation by our Lord Jesus Christ" (1 Thessalonians 1:10; 5:9).

Jacob Marcellus Kik writes in his book, *An Eschatology of Victory* (The Presbyterian and Reformed Publishing Company, 1971, pp. 96-97):

> "One of the most remarkable things about the siege of Jerusalem was the miraculous escape of Christians. It has been estimated that over a million Jews lost their lives in that terrible siege, but not one of them was a Christian. This our Lord indicated in verse 13: 'But he that shall endure to the end, the same shall be saved.' That the 'end' spoken of was not the termination of a Christian's life but rather the end of Jerusalem is evident from the context. Immediately after this verse Christ goes on to relate the exact time of the end. Christians who would live to the end would be saved from the terrible tribulation. Christ indicates also the time for the Christian to flee from the city so that he could be saved during its destruction. This is verified in a parallel passage (Luke 21:18): 'But there shall not an hair of your head perish.' In other words, during the desolation of Jerusalem, Christians would be unharmed, although in the period previous to this some would lose their lives through persecution."

Jesus said to His disciples that "They shall put you out of the synagogues: yea, the time cometh, that whosoever [kills] you will think that he [does] God a service" (John 16:2). Jesus had already warned His disciples that they would be killed and crucified and scourged and persecuted; so how can He also say, "not a hair of your head shall perish?"

Many would die because of their testimony and the persecution they would endure. That is why we see the "souls of them that were slain for the Word of God and for the testimony which they held" (Revelation 6:9). These were the ones who came out of great tribulation and who are arrayed in white robes (Revelation 7:13-14).

They were not partakers of the wrath of God's judgment, but those who died because of the persecution Jesus warned His disciples about. Many others who were sealed by God were saved as they fled the city of Jerusalem, when they saw, "Jerusalem compassed with armies (Luke 21:20-21).

Chapter seven continues with the sealing of the 144,000. Again, this number represents all believers, which is indicated here by the 12,000 out of each of the twelve tribes of Israel (12,000 x 12); but the product is, "a great multitude, which no man could number, of all nations, and kindreds, and people, and tongues" (Revelation 7:9).

We might also notice that the twelve tribes mentioned here are not the twelve tribes of Israel, as are listed in other places in Scripture. Here, Joseph is mentioned as a tribe, but Dan and Ephraim are conspicuously missing. The first believers were all Jewish, and were of the twelve tribes.

Later, the Gentiles (non-Jews) were evangelized, and they came into the Church, but they were also included in the promises to Abraham and his seed, which made up the tribes:

> ...For as many of you as have been baptized into Christ have put on Christ. There is neither Jew nor Greek, there is neither bond nor free, there is neither male nor female: for [you] are all one in Christ Jesus. And if [you] be Christ's, then are [you] Abraham's seed, and heirs according to the promise (Galatians 3:27-29).

In chapter eight, the seventh seal is broken and there is a half-hour of silence in heaven; followed by seven angels who are given trumpets. Another angel appears with a golden censer and much incense, to offer it with the prayers of the saints upon the golden altar, which was before the throne.

This is reminiscent of the hour of prayer that was to take place in the Temple each day. The people would gather in the outer court of the Temple in the morning and the evening, to pray, while a priest would take a hot coal from off of the altar and carry it into the first section of the Temple, called the holy place. In front of the veil was a golden altar of incense where he would place the hot coal; then he would sprinkle incense on the coal to create a fragrant smoke that would filter beyond the veil and before the throne of God.

Offering the incense would take about a half an hour, as the people prayed in silence in the outer court. The incense smoke represented the prayers of the saints. This outer court was the same area Jesus cleansed on two occasions when He turned over the tables of the currency brokers, and drove out the animals that were being sold for sacrifice.

Jesus said, "My house shall be called the house of prayer; but [you] have made it a den of thieves" (Matthew 21:13). This would also have been the assignment Zacharias had when the angel spoke to him about the birth of his son, John the Baptist (Luke 1:8-11).

It would seem that the actions of the angel of God, who filled the censer with fire and cast it upon the land, was in response to the prayers of the saints who were enduring much persecution. This action of the angel resulted in voices, thundering, lightning, and an earthquake. God is sending the seven angels to blow the trumpets that will release the wrath of God's judgment against the persecutors.

Chapter 9

Seven Trumpets

WHEN THE FIRST FOUR ANGELS sound the trumpets, plagues are released in the land, that seem to mimic the plagues against Pharaoh and Egypt in the days of Moses (Exodus 7:20; 9:24; 10:21). Hail, fire, blood, bitter waters, and darkness are all associated with the trumpets that announce God's judgment.

The "star" called Wormwood that fell upon the rivers and fountains and that caused the water to become bitter, is not a new symbol. Jeremiah uses the term "wormwood" to express the bitterness of God's judgment on the rebellious (Jeremiah 9:15; 23:15; Lamentations 3:15,19). The prophet Amos makes use of this term in reference to the unrighteous judges who "turn judgment to wormwood" (Amos 5:7).

When the fifth angel blows his trumpet, we see a star fall from heaven, who opens the abyss; releasing unworldly locusts that brought torment to those without the seal of God. We have already seen stars falling from heaven, which represent the ruin of rulers, kings, or kingdoms.

Daniel prophesied of a leader who would rise up against Israel (the pleasant land) and "...cast down *some* of the host and *some* of the stars to the ground, and trampled them..." (Daniel 8:9-10

NKJV). Obviously, these are not celestial stars, but rulers. And one result of this leader's rising would be that the daily sacrifice in the Temple would be taken away and the sanctuary (Temple) would be cast down.

Here are two very interesting historical facts about a wicked ruler who unleashes much torment upon Jerusalem, for a period of five months.

First, the terrorizing of the Jewish leaders in Jerusalem by the Roman procurator of Judea, Gessius Florus, lasted for a period of five months, according to Flavius Josephus: (*The Wars of the Jews*, book 2; chpt. 14; sect.9 to chpt. 19; sect. 9). This event is recorded as being the catalyst that began the Jewish war with Rome. The excuse Gessius used to scourge and crucify over three thousand Jewish leaders in Jerusalem was that they ceased to offer the daily sacrifice for the emperor. (This event was already discussed in chapter six of this book).

Secondly, the siege by the future Roman Emperor Titus began in April of A.D. 70 and lasted for five months, until the city of Jerusalem and the Temple were both destroyed. With the destruction of the Temple, the daily sacrifices ceased.

I am not suggesting that either Gessius Florus or Titus were demonic angels, but only that the symbolism here in *Revelation 9* speaks to an unleashing of terror and torment by both the Roman armies, and the Jewish rebel factions. The actions of the Zealots, as described by Josephus, are nothing less than total insanity and demon possession. Here is what Josephus writes about their actions:

> "With their insatiable hunger for loot, they ransacked the houses of the wealthy, murdered men and violated women for sport; they drank their spoils with blood, and

from mere satiety they shamelessly gave themselves up to effeminate practices, plaiting their hair and putting on women's clothes, drenching themselves with perfumes and painting their eyelids to make themselves attractive. They copied not merely the dress, but also the passions of women, devising in their excess of licentiousness unlawful pleasures in which they wallowed as in a brothel. Thus they entirely polluted the city with their foul practices. Yet though they wore women's faces, their hands were murderous. They would approach with mincing steps, then suddenly become fighting men, and, whipping out their swords from under their dyed cloaks, they would run through every passerby." (In: *The Works of Josephus:* New Updated Edition. Copyright 1987 by Hendrickson Publisher, Inc.; *The Wars of the Jews*; book 4; chat. 9; sect. 10).

The insanity of the Jewish factions that had no organized defense provoked the strongest military force in history; and as a result, they suffered indescribable torments. Such madness could only be provoked by the flood of demonic deception ruled by Apollyon, the Destroyer. This account of the five months of torment is called the first "woe," and it is followed with a warning of two more woes that will follow (Revelation 9:12).

The sixth angel sounded the trumpet, and John heard a voice from the four horns of the golden altar, which is before God (Revelation 9:13). The sixth angel was instructed to "loose" the four angels that were bound in the river Euphrates. Historically, the Euphrates was the boundary between Israel and the many enemy armies that invaded them.

The Assyrians, Babylonians, and the Persians all crossed the Euphrates with their armies, to fight against Israel. Some translations give the number of the invading armies as two hundred million; but the word in Greek means "myriads," which is an innumerable company – literally two myriads of horsemen. This same word is used in *Luke 12:1*, where it says "an innumerable number of people" gathered to hear Jesus. In other words, there were many.

We must remember that John is seeing things that are happening both in the spirit, and in the earthly realms. From the spiritual perspective, we see these four angels (messengers) riding lion-headed, fire-breathing horses, with venomous serpent-like tails. From an earthly perspective, there were four battalions of Roman soldiers based at the Euphrates River. They had received their orders from Cestius, who commissioned them to march down the Jordan valley and through the cities of Galilee; destroying every Jewish township and village along the way to Jerusalem.

The tenth chapter of *Revelation* contains the voice of the seventh angel, who sounds his trumpet and declares that, "…the mystery of God should be finished, as he [has] declared to his servants the prophets" (Revelation 10:7). What is the mystery of God? Well, according to Paul, it is the gospel of the Lord Jesus Christ:

> Now to him that is of power to establish you according to my gospel, and the preaching of Jesus Christ, according to the revelation of the mystery, which was kept secret since the world began, But now is made manifest, and by the scriptures of the prophets, according to the commandment of the everlasting God, made known to all nations for the obedience of faith (Romans 16:25-26).

> And for me, that utterance may be given unto me, that I may open my mouth boldly, to make known the mystery of the gospel (Ephesians 6:19).

Even the mystery which has been hid from ages and from generations, but now is made manifest to his saints: To whom God would make known what is the riches of the glory of this mystery among the Gentiles; which is Christ in you, the hope of glory (Colossians 1:26-27).

The mystery of the ages was that "Christ in you" is "the hope of glory." The Jews who worshiped God (Jehovah), and the pagans who worshiped their gods, each had a temple or a place to go and worship. They had a place to bring their sacrifices and fulfill their prescribed means of worship, to appease their god; hoping for their god's presence and blessings to be upon them because of their sacrifice.

But the gospel of Jesus Christ was different. The one who believed in the sacrifice of Jesus on the cross became the Temple of God. The worshiper pleased God by faith in the self-sacrifice Jesus completed. As a result, the worshiper becomes the place of the presence of God. Believers no longer try to appease God for sin with some kind of gift; but they receive not only forgiveness for sin, but a new life that is transformed by the abiding presence of God.

The fulfillment of this mystery is seen in the destruction of the stone Temple in Jerusalem. God will never again dwell in any Temple made by the hands of men. "Do you not know that you are God's temple and that God's Spirit dwells in you?" (1 Corinthians 3:16 ESV).

The remainder of chapter ten involves a "little book" that lies open in the hands of the angel who has just declared that there would be no more delay in fulfilling the mystery. John was instructed to go to the angel and take the book from his hand and eat it up. It would be as sweet as honey in his mouth, but bitter in his belly. As a result, John would prophesy before "many peoples, and nations, and tongues, and kings" (Revelation 10:11).

This reminds us of *Psalm 19:7-10*, where David proclaims that the Word of God is sweeter than "honey and the honeycomb." Although the words of prophecy in the little book are sweet to John's taste; his belly becomes bitter because of the coming judgment he will yet proclaim.

Chapter eleven begins with John being given a rod to measure the Temple. He is told to only measure the Temple of God and the altar, and those who are worshiping there; but not the outer court, which shall be "given to the Gentiles, and they will trample the holy city for forty-two months" (Revelation 11:1-2 NET).

The act of measuring the Temple is found in several places in the Bible.

> The Lord has rejected His altar,
> He has repudiated His sanctuary;
> He has handed over
> The walls of her palaces to the enemy.
> They have made a noise in the house of the LORD
> As on the day of an appointed feast.
> The LORD determined to destroy
> The wall of the daughter of Zion.
> He has stretched out a line,
> He has not restrained His hand from destroying,
> And He has caused rampart and wall to mourn;
> They have languished together.
> Her gates have sunk into the ground,
> He has destroyed and broken her bars
> (Lamentations 2:7-9 NASB).

So He showed me, and behold, the Lord was standing by a vertical wall with a plumb line in His hand. Then the LORD said, "What do you see, Amos?" And I said, "A plumb line." Then the Lord said, "Behold I am about to put a plumb line in the midst of My people Israel. I will not spare them any longer. The high places of Isaac will become deserted, And the sanctuaries of Israel will be in ruins… (Amos 7:7-9 NASB).

…therefore this is what the LORD, the God of Israel says: 'Behold, I am bringing *such a* disaster on Jerusalem and Judah that whoever hears about it, both of his ears will ring. I will stretch over Jerusalem the line of Samaria and the plummet of the house of Ahab, and I will wipe Jerusalem clean just as one wipes a bowl, wiping it and turning it upside down. And I will abandon the remnant of My inheritance and hand them over to their enemies, and they will become as plunder and spoils to all their enemies (2 Kings 21:12-14 NASB).

Each of these Scriptures refer to a time in Israel's history when God measured the city of Jerusalem and the people there; and as a result, He handed them over to their enemies to be destroyed. As the city was measured for destruction, so the Temple John was given to measure was devoted to destruction. The outer court and the city were given to the Gentiles (Romans) to be trampled down for forty-two months. This is the same time that Jesus spoke of when He said:

But when you see Jerusalem surrounded by armies, then know that its desolation is near. And they will fall by the edge of the sword and be led away captive into all nations. And Jerusalem will be trampled by Gentiles until the times of the Gentiles are fulfilled (Luke 21:20,24 NKJV).

This is the same kind of "measuring" mentioned in the *Book of Daniel*. Belshazzar, the king of Babylon, had profaned the articles of worship taken from the Temple in Jerusalem by his grandfather Nebuchadnezzar. He sent for the gold and silver cups from the Temple, to use at his feast to praise the gods of gold, silver, brass, iron, stone, and wood (Daniel 5:4).

Fingers of a man's hand appeared and wrote a message on the wall of the palace. When none of the kings' advisors could interpret the writing, the king summoned Daniel to the feast to interpret the meaning. Daniel then told the king the meaning, "…God has numbered your kingdom, and finished it… You are weighed in the balances, and found wanting" (Daniel 5:5,26-27). That very night, King Belshazzar was slain, and Darius the Mede seized the kingdom.

John is shown that the city of Jerusalem and the outer court of the Temple will be overrun by the Romans (Gentiles) for forty-two months. John was given the job of measuring the Temple (the holy place), the altar (where prayers were presented on the golden altar of incense), and those who worship there (the priests).

Why is John "measuring" this holy place, and the priests? What is in the "holy place" where only the priests (the descendants of Aaron) could enter? When the priest entered the "holy place," he would see in this windowless room, the table of showbread on his right. On that table were twelve loaves of bread. To the left, the priest would see the seven branched lampstand made of gold, and the seven oil lamps it held, which supplied the only light in the room.

At the back of the room was the veil that separated the holy place from the most holy place, which housed the Ark of the Covenant. In front of the veil was the golden altar of incense, where every morning and every evening, a priest would bring in a censor, a hot coal from the brazen altar. That altar was outside in the court, where animal sacrifices were made.

The priest would place the hot coal on the golden altar before the veil, and sprinkle incense on the hot coal, which created a fragrant smoke that would filter beyond the veil into the most holy place of God's presence. If the purpose of "measuring" this place and the priests that ministered there was for destruction as we have seen in other Scriptures; then why is this place and its processes condemned? The answer may be seen in the following Scriptures.

Immediately following the angel's instructions to John to measure the Temple, is the description of the two witnesses. They are appointed to prophesy for 1,260 days, clothed in sackcloth. They are identified as "…the two olive trees and the two lampstands that stand before the Lord of the earth" (Revelation 11:4 NET). Now, we can either guess about what or who these witnesses are, or we can go to the Scriptures and find out.

In the *Book of Zechariah*, we find a lampstand, two olive trees, and two anointed ones, "who stand by the Lord of the whole earth." The prophet Zechariah is prophesying to Joshua the high priest, and Zerubbabel the governor. These Jewish leaders had been sent from Babylon to rebuild the Temple at Jerusalem.

The first Temple was built by King Solomon, the son of David. Centuries later, the Babylonians destroyed the Temple and the city of Jerusalem; and took the Jewish people into exile for seventy years. During those seventy years, the Persians defeated the Babylonians. In the first year of king Cyrus of Persia, a decree was made for the Jews to return to Jerusalem and to rebuild the Temple. Joshua, the high priest, and Zerubbabel, the governor, returned; accompanied by about 50,000 Jews.

In Jerusalem, they encountered many threats by their enemies, as well as shortages and betrayals. Even after they laid the foundation of this second Temple, they were forced to stop the construction for about fifteen years. To encourage Joshua and Zerubbabel, God gave the prophet Zechariah a vision regarding the completion of the Temple. Zechariah saw a seven-branched lampstand with a bowl above it, and seven pipes from it that supplied the oil to the lamps. On either side of the lampstand were two olive trees; and from them were two golden pipes that continuously filled the bowl with oil.

When Zechariah asked the angel about the meaning of the two olive trees, the bowl, and the seven lamps, the angel answered and said, "This is the word of the LORD unto Zerubbabel, saying, Not by might, nor by power, but by my spirit, saith the LORD of hosts" (Zechariah 4:6). Zechariah then asked the angel, "What are these two olive branches?" and he was told, "These are the two anointed ones, that stand by the LORD of the whole earth" (Zechariah 4:12,14).

Now, how does the story in *Zechariah* fit with the eleventh chapter of *Revelation*? First, the Temple in *Revelation* is measured for destruction. Jesus spoke of the buildings of the Temple and said, "There shall not be left here one stone upon another, that shall not be thrown down" (Matthew 24:2). That beautiful stone Temple was about to be destroyed by the Romans. The Old Testament Temple, priesthood, and animal sacrifices were being done away with (Hebrews 8:13). In their place was a new Temple; not made with men's hands but by the Spirit of God.

Jesus is building His Church (Matthew 16:18) and His Church is the new Temple Jesus inhabits by the Holy Spirit (John 14:17,23; 1 Corinthians 3:16; 6:19). The foundation upon which this Temple is built is *the revelation that Jesus is the Messiah*

(Christ) (Matthew 16:16-17). Everyone who believes is like a "living stone" built upon the sure foundation of the revelation that Jesus is Lord (1 Peter 2:5; Isaiah 28:16).

This foundation for the spiritual Temple Jesus is building is also found in the *Book of Zechariah*. We have seen in chapter four, that Zerubbabel, the governor, will complete the building of the Temple, but not by his might or power, but by the Spirit of the Lord (Zechariah 4:6-9).

In chapter three, the vision Zechariah receives is about Joshua the high priest. He sees Joshua clothed in filthy garments; but there are instructions given to remove his filthy garments and give him clean ones. "See, I have removed your iniquity from you, and I will clothe you with rich robes" (Zechariah 3:4 NKJV). The Lord then says to Joshua:

> ...Hear now, O Joshua the high priest... I will bring forth my servant the Branch. For behold the stone that I have laid before Joshua; upon one stone shall be seven eyes: behold, I will engrave the graving thereof, saith the Lord of hosts, and I will remove the iniquity of that land in one day (Zechariah 3:8-9).

Both Joshua the High Priest, and Zerubbabel the governmental ruling authority (king) are types of the Lord Jesus, who is both High Priest and King (Hebrews 3:1,4:14; Revelation 1:5; 19:16). Just as these two men were building the Temple of God in Jerusalem; so Jesus is building His Temple/Church.

Jesus is also identified as the "Branch." Throughout the writings of the Old Testament prophets, we see this term regarding the one who would come, remove iniquity, and build His Temple (Isaiah 11:1-2; Jeremiah 23:5-6; Zechariah 6:12). The stone with "seven eyes" is a "living stone," as mentioned in 1 Peter 2:4. He will remove iniquity in one day and build His Church (Temple). These Scriptures obviously speak of the redemptive work of the Lord Jesus Christ. And it is interesting that the names Joshua and Jesus are the same (Joshua from Hebrew, and Jesus from the Greek).

Jesus had pronounced destruction upon the city of Jerusalem and the Temple when the religious rulers rejected Him (Matthew 23:35-37). Now, at the end of Jesus' three and one-half-year ministry, He would be killed, just as the two witnesses were killed, who had prophesied 1,260 days (three and one-half years). But are these two witnesses literally two men, or do they just represent the testimony of the Word of God from the Law and the Prophets?

Although the names of these witnesses are missing, their works may reveal their identity. We know that Moses turned water into blood and brought forth the plagues upon Egypt after Pharaoh refused to let Israel go. We know that Elijah prayed that it would not rain and there was a drought for three and one-half years, and that Elijah also called fire down upon his enemies (Exodus 7:17-20; 1 Kings 17:1; 2 Kings 1:10; James 5:17).

These are the same works of the two witnesses in *Revelation*. Also, the two witnesses are identified as the two lampstands and olive trees; represented by Joshua and Zerubbabel, the builders of the second Temple. These two men, Moses and Elijah, may represent more than God's prophets in their day. They represent the Law and the Prophets, which give witness to, and are fulfilled in the Lord Jesus, as the following Scriptures show us.

> "…We have found him, of whom Moses in the law, and the prophets, did write, Jesus of Nazareth, the son of Joseph" (John 1:45).

"But now the righteousness of God without the law is manifested, being witnessed by the Law and the Prophets" (Romans 3:21).

Jesus said, "Do not think I came to destroy the Law or the Prophets. I did not come to destroy but to fulfill" (Matthew 5:17 PARAPHRASED).

These Scriptures identify the Law and the Prophets, as two witnesses of the Lord Jesus, and what He would do. Daniel had prophesied that after 483 years from the commandment to rebuild the city of Jerusalem, that certain things would happen: "…finish the transgression…make an end of sins…reconciliation for iniquity… bring in everlasting righteousness, and to seal (bring about the vision and prophesy [EXB]) and to anoint the most Holy" (Daniel 9:24). All of these things were fulfilled by Jesus within the three and one-half year time frame of His ministry.

It was also Moses and Elijah who appeared with Jesus on the Mount of Transfiguration; and who "spoke of His "decease" (death), which He was about to accomplish at Jerusalem" (Luke 9:28-31 NKJV).

If Jesus was the fulfillment of God's Word, of all that the Law and the Prophets had declared; then when He was crucified, it would appear that God's Word had failed. The Law and the Prophets (Moses and Elijah) died; and the enemies of God rejoiced of the broken covenant (represented by both three and one-half years, and three and one-half days).[5]

---

[5] Three and one-half in Scripture is a broken seven, with seven being fulfillment, completion, or perfection. Half of seven is often seen as incomplete, broken, or unfulfilled, as is seen in *Daniel 9:27*. The three and one-half time frame is referred to throughout the Scriptures, and which is expressed as three and one-half years, forty-two months, 1,260 days, and times, times, and the dividing of times. All of these reference a time of trouble and Israel's judgment for the broken covenant with God, as seen in Elijah's word: that it would not rain for three and one-half years, or the judgment against Israel for forty-two months, as Rome destroyed the city and the Temple.

The enemies of God had always attempted to stop the fulfillment of God's promise to man, regarding the "seed of the woman," who would crush the head of the serpent (Genesis 3:15). But those enemies were deceived to believe that killing Jesus would end God's plan for man's redemption. It was a hidden mystery to them, as Paul declares,

> But we speak the wisdom of God in a mystery, even the hidden wisdom, which God ordained before the world unto our glory: Which none of the princes of this world knew: for had they known it, they would not have crucified the Lord of glory (1 Corinthians 2:7-8).

Those who rejoiced in the death of God's Word would soon discover their mistake, "But after the three and a half days a breath of life from God entered them, and they stood up on their feet, and great fear fell on those who saw them" (Revelation 11:11 ESV).

All that the Law and the Prophets had declared was fulfilled; not only when Jesus died, but when He was resurrected and "…ascended up to heaven in a cloud" (Revelation 11:12). This sounds a lot like, "…while they beheld, he was taken up; and a cloud received him out of their sight." (Acts 1:9).

The remainder of chapter eleven includes the continued destruction as a great earthquake kills seven thousand men and destroys a tenth of the city. The seventh trumpet sounds; fulfilling the mystery of God, which we discussed earlier: that Christ now lives in His Church, not a Temple made by man (Revelation 10:7). Then, a decree was heard in heaven, saying, "The kingdoms of this world are become the kingdoms of our Lord, and of his Christ; and he shall reign for ever and ever" (Revelation 11:15). The "prince of this world" has had his head crushed, as Jesus "destroyed the works of the devil" (1 John 3:8).

The nations were angry, as God stirred up wrath against those who were corrupting the land (Israel). The Romans were destroying the inhabitants of Jerusalem, and all of the Jewish cities. Jesus had warned that judgment was coming to Chorazin, Bethsaida, and Capernaum (Matthew 11:21-22). This was the time of the dead to be judged, and the reward of the slain prophets and saints that are mentioned in the opening of the fifth seal (Revelation 6:9-11).

This is not the final judgment of the end of days, but the vindication of the martyred saints – the judgment that Jesus said would come upon that generation (Matthew 24:34)! The last verse of this chapter shows us that the Temple was opened in heaven, and there, the Ark of the Covenant is seen. The man-made stone Temple in Jerusalem is destroyed on the earth, and the true Temple is revealed in heaven.

With the redemptive work of Jesus being completed, God tore the veil separating man from God, and gave us access into the true heavenly Temple in the heavenly Jerusalem (Matthew 27:51; Ephesians 2:19-22; Hebrews 4:16; 8:1-6; 9:8; 10:19-22).

Chapter 10

Signs in the Heavens

REVELATION 12 GIVES A SPIRITUAL perspective of the historical events from the birth of Jesus; His victorious spiritual warfare; His defeating the devil; and His death, resurrection, and ascension.

First, there is a sign in heaven of a woman clothed with the sun. She has the moon under her feet and a crown of twelve stars upon her head. She is pregnant and ready to give birth to a "man child," who will "rule the nations with a rod of iron" (Revelation 12:5). Standing before her is a "great red dragon," with seven heads and ten horns that is ready to devour her child, as soon as He is born. It is not difficult to see the meaning behind what these symbols represent. This imagery depicts the woman who gives birth to a child, who is to rule all nations with a rod of iron.

> …I have set My King
> On my holy hill of Zion.
> I will declare the decree:
> The LORD has said to Me,
> You *are* My Son,
> Today I have begotten You.
> Ask of Me, and I shall give *You*
> The nations *for* Your inheritance,

And the ends of the earth *for* Your possession.
You shall break them with a rod of iron;
You shall dash them in pieces like a potter's vessel (Psalms 2:6-9 NKJV).

Now out of His mouth goes a sharp sword, that with it He should strike the nations. And He Himself will rule them with a rod of iron (Revelation 19:15 NKJV).

This "man child" is obviously the Lord Jesus, who is born of Mary (Matthew 1:16), but here, the woman represents not just Mary, but Israel as a nation or kingdom. This symbolism shows the woman with the sun, moon, and stars, representing a kingdom as discussed in chapter 1 of this book. This kingdom is identified by the twelve stars (tribes of Israel) through whom would come the Seed of the woman, seed of Abraham, the Messiah, Savior, and Son of God (Genesis 3:15; Hebrews 2:16).

The great red dragon is clearly identified as "…that old serpent, called the Devil, and Satan, which deceives the whole world" (Revelation 12:9 PARAPHRASED). We have already seen the fourth beast described to Daniel as the fourth kingdom (Rome); and that the ten horns are kings or rulers that witnessed another horn (king) who would rise up and who "made war with the saints and prevailed against them" (Daniel 7:21).

Don't be confused that this horn or king is also referring to the devil or Satan, the ancient serpent. The king (Nero) is identified with the devil. Nero the man is not the devil, but he is used of the devil to accomplish his purposes. We have already discussed how Satan uses the authority of man (Adam) to enforce his will. He cannot steal, destroy, and kill, apart from finding someone he can work through.

This king (Emperor Nero), as we have seen, brings great persecution against the saints, for a period of three and one-half years; and initiates the Roman war against the Jews (also for a period of three and one-half years). That ends with the destruction of both the city of Jerusalem and the Temple (chapter 5 of this book). We have also seen God's protection for the saints who fled Jerusalem when they saw the city "compassed with armies" (Luke 21:20), as Jesus told them to do.

All throughout the Old Testament Scriptures, the devil has attempted to destroy the promised "Seed of the woman" (Genesis 3:15). Cain, the wicked one, kills Abel, the righteous one. Whether it was the Egyptian rulers attempting to kill all the baby boys of the Hebrews; or King Herod slaying all of the male babies in Bethlehem, this demonic dragon has influenced the kings of nations to destroy the Jews – for it was through this nation that brought forth the seed of Abraham, that the dragon slayer would be born (Galatians 3:16).

As this woman flees to the wilderness, where she is protected for 1,260 days (three and one-half years), so Christians fled from Jerusalem and were protected from the judgment of God upon Israel, at the hands of the Romans. The dragon continued "to make war with the remnant of her Seed, which…have the testimony of Jesus" (Revelation 12:17). These saints overcame the dragon by the "blood of the Lamb, and by the word of their testimony; and they loved not their lives unto the death" (Revelation 12:11).

Revelation 12 has one more thing we want to consider. The devil drew a third part of the stars of heaven, and did cast them into the earth. I have heard many times that this passage of Scripture references the devil taking one-third of the angels, who followed him in his rebellion against God. But is that what this Scripture really means?

Is there any Scripture that speaks of a third of the angels following Satan in his rebellion? I do not find any. The stars of heaven are most often represented by the children of Israel. The promise to Abraham and Isaac was that their "seed" would be multiplied "as the "stars of heaven." Take a look at these examples from Scripture:

> That in blessing I will bless [you], and in multiplying I will multiply [your] seed as the stars of the heaven (Genesis 22:17).

> "And I will make [your] seed to multiply as the stars of heaven" (Genesis 26:4).

> "Remember Abraham, Isaac, and Israel, [your] servants, to whom [you] sware by [your] own self, and [said] unto them, I will multiply your seed as the stars of heaven" (Exodus 32:13).

> The LORD your God [has] multiplied you, and behold, [you] are this day as the stars of heaven for multitude (Deuteronomy 1:10).

In *Daniel 8:10*, we read about a vision that Daniel had when he was at the palace in Shushan; during the reign of Belshazzar, who was the last king of Babylon. In this vision, Daniel saw a ram with two horns; and then a goat with one "notable" horn, that ran into the ram and broke both his horns. The goat reigned until his great horn was broken, and in its place, four horns came up. Then, a little horn came up that pushed against the east, the south, and the land of Israel, until it became great; even against the host of heaven, "and it cast down some of the host" of heaven, "and of the stars to the ground," and trampled on them.

The point here is that he "cast down some of the host and of the stars to the ground, and trampled on them." Daniel did not understand the vision, so God sent the angel Gabriel to explain its meaning. The ram with two horns represents the kings of the Medes and Persians. The goat is the king of Greece. After the goat's great horn is broken, four other horns (kings) come up in its place. From one of those kings would come one who would attempt to destroy the people of God, and come against the Prince of princes, but he shall not succeed.

Looking back in history, it is easy to understand this vision that was explained to Daniel. The Babylonians were defeated by the Medes and Persians (the two-horned ram). A king of the Greeks (the goat with one horn) would defeat them – that was Alexander the Great. When the goat died (his horn was broken), four horns or kings came up in his place. After Alexander died, his four generals divided his empire.

Two of these were important to Daniel's vision. Ptolemy was given control over Palestine and Egypt. Seleucus controlled Asia Minor, Syria, and Mesopotamia. Eventually, one of the Seleucid kings, Antiochus IV Epiphanes (175 to 164 B.C.) made war against a Ptolemic king and defeated him; taking control of the land of Israel. In his zeal to expand Greek culture and worship of the Greek gods, he entered the Temple in Jerusalem and set up a statue of Jupiter in the Most Holy Place. He caused the daily sacrifice to cease and desecrated the altar by offering a pig.

The Jews raised arms against him, which was known as the "Wars of the Maccabees." These conflicts and their outcomes are well-documented in the four books of the Maccabees, and by the historian Josephus.

This event took place in the second century before Jesus was born, but we can see that the symbolism is much the same as found in *Revelation*. The "little horn" that fought against the people of God to destroy them, is seen casting some of the host and stars to the ground, to trample them; much like the dragon who "draws" a third of the stars and casts them to the earth (ground).

This is *not* the devil convincing a third of the angels to rebel against God; but this "casting down" is to destroy the people of God (Revelation 12:4). The dragon is "casting down" the stars. The language here, as in *Daniel 8*, conveys the idea of a violent throwing down, and not a persuasion to follow.

This violent casting down is the same in *Revelation 12:9*, where the dragon was cast out with his angels. Yes, there are "fallen" or rebellious angels who followed Satan and were cast out of heaven; but we do not know how many there were. Notice that the war in heaven in verse 7 results in the devil losing his place and being "cast out" or "cast down" from heaven; where he, as the "accuser of our brethren…accused them before our God day and night" (Revelation 12:10).

When was the devil cast out of heaven? It was just prior to Jesus going to the cross. He said, "Now is the judgment of this world: now shall the prince of this world be cast out" (John 12:31). "The prince of the power of the air" (Ephesians 2:2), or ruler, or "god of this world" (2 Corinthians 4:4) is the devil.

What did he do? He accused the brethren before God, day and night. But with the cross and the resurrection, Jesus, the "man child" who was "caught up unto God, and his throne" (Revelation 12:5) paid the price for man's forgiveness and redemption; now the devil has no more access to God to accuse man. At the cross of Jesus, the price was *paid in full* for mankind's redemption; and with the resurrection of Jesus, the devil was defeated. *Revelation 12* is a review of all that Jesus accomplished for us.

Chapter thirteen of the *Book of Revelation* reveals two beasts. One rises out of the sea, and another out of the land.

The description of the first beast is very familiar. He had seven heads, ten horns, and crowns upon his horns; and on his heads, the names of blasphemy. And his appearance was like a leopard, a bear, and a lion. The dragon gave him his power, his throne, and his authority.

We have seen this beast before in *Daniel 7:2-7*, and we see it again in *Revelation 17:3,7*. His description is much like that of the dragon in *Revelation 12:3*. Again, the dragon (devil) gives power to the kings and kingdoms (beasts) of this world, to do his will and to destroy the people of God.

When Jesus was tempted in the wilderness, we are told, "Then the devil, taking Him up on a high mountain, showed Him all the kingdoms of the world in a moment of time. And the devil said to Him, "All this authority I will give You, and their glory; for *this* has been delivered to me, and I give it to whomever I wish. Therefore, if You will worship before me, all will be Yours." (Luke 4:5-7 NKJV). Jesus came to defeat the devil and restore the kingdoms of this world to God.

This beast is a *composite* of all of the previous kingdoms mentioned in *Daniel*. These things are happening during the time of the Roman Empire (the diverse beast), but this has elements of the three previous kingdoms of the leopard (Greeks), the bear (Medes and Persians), and the lion (Babylonian).

As the people of God (the Church) are to carry the image and likeness of God; so these wicked kings and kingdoms carry the image and likeness of the dragon. One of the heads of this beast was wounded unto death, but it appears as if the deadly wound was healed. What did Jesus come to do? He came to crush the head of the serpent (dragon), who controls the nations. Jesus "destroyed him who had the power of death, that is, the devil and deliver them who through the fear of death were all their lifetime subject to bondage" (Hebrews 2:14-15 PARAPHRASED).

Jesus defeated the devil, rose again, ascended to heaven, and empowered His Church to establish the kingdom of God in the earth. But it appears that the wounding unto death of the kingdoms of the world – culminating in Rome – is healed. Rome is strong; it blasphemes God and demands worship; and it persecutes believers and makes war with the saints.

The second beast came up out of the earth (land). As has been mentioned before, the "land" is always in reference to Israel. Israel was the "Land of Promise." When the people obeyed God, they dwelt safely in the land and were blessed and protected from their enemies. When they disobeyed God, they were removed out of the land, and were ruled over by their enemies. But here, in verse 11, another "beast" comes up out of the land. It looks like a lamb, but it speaks like the dragon. It came out of the land of Israel, but it was in league with the dragon and the first beast (Rome), to destroy the people of God.

While the Jewish multitudes gladly received Jesus, the Jewish leadership constantly opposed Him and looked for an opportunity to kill Him (Mark 3:6; Luke 22:2; John 19:6,15). The first persecution against the Church came from the Jewish leadership Acts 4:6,18; 12:1-3; 17:5; 18:12.

Jesus had warned about false prophets that would arise, but who were only wolves in sheep's clothing (Matthew 7:15). There were many false prophets who did miracles, and Israel and the Church were warned not to believe them (Deuteronomy 13:1; Matthew 24:5,11; Acts 13:6-11).

This land beast (false prophet) deceives the people to honor and reverence the first beast (Rome/Nero), by creating an image, a statue of him to be worshipped. We have already discussed how Nero himself was referred to as a "beast," and how the Emperor of Rome was acknowledged as the personification of the Roman state. Thus, Nero and Rome are the same; Nero, the puppet of the dragon, who demanded to be worshiped as a god.

The Roman emperors took on the title of deity. They called themselves "Augustus" or "Sebastes," meaning "one to be worshiped." Nero demanded absolute obedience. He erected a 120-foot-tall statue of himself, and instituted "Emperor Worship," requiring the subjects of Rome to go to the city square, where they resided, and sprinkled incense on an "eternal flame," while declaring that "Caesar is Lord."

These very actions are described by the Apostle Paul, who wrote to the Thessalonian Church regarding the "man of sin… the son of perdition, who opposes and exalts himself above all that is called God or that is worshiped, so that he sits as God in the temple of God, showing himself that he is God" (2 Thessalonians 2:3-4 NKJV).

Nero fits the bill as the beast:…speaking great things and blasphemies … blasphemy against God, to blaspheme his name, and his tabernacle, and them that dwell in heaven" and he made "war with the saints" and overcame them for forty-two months (three and one-half years), and was given authority over all "kindreds, and tongues, and nations" (Revelation 13:5-7 PARAPHRASED). Rome ruled the world, and Nero thought himself to be a god who ruled the nations.

The remainder of this chapter deals with the beast and the mark in the right hand or the forehead, that all were required to receive, in order to buy or sell. The last verse emphasizes again, the number of the beast, which is the number of the man, and which is 666 (Revelation 13:18). We have already discussed this mark in detail, in chapter 5 of this book.

Chapter 11

The Grapes Are Ready for Harvest

REVELATION 14 BEGINS WITH THE Lamb on mount Zion, with 144,000 having the name of the Father in their foreheads. This contrasts with those who give allegiance to the beast, and who carry his mark. The Lamb (Jesus) is with the people of God, the 144,000 (12,000 x 12). These represent all those who follow Christ. They are virgins; that is, they have not committed spiritual adultery with the beast, by declaring that Caesar is "Lord."

Next are six angels (messengers). The first messenger brings the gospel to the nations of peoples living in the land of Israel. Remember that Israel is a melting pot of Jews who come from all over the world.

> And how hear we every man in our own tongue, wherein we were born? Parthians, and Medes, and Elamites, and the dwellers in Mesopotamia, and in Judea, and Cappadocia, in Pontus and Asia, Phrygia, and Pamphylia, in Egypt, and in the parts of Libya about Cyrene, and strangers of Rome, Jews and proselytes, Cretes and Arabians, we

do hear them speak in our tongues the wonderful works of God (Acts 2:8-11).

The first angel encourages the people to worship God and know that the time of judgment has come. This is "good news" to those Christians who are suffering great persecution. This judgment is not the judgment of the last day at the resurrection, but the promised judgment upon "this generation." when Jerusalem and the Temple would be destroyed. This judgment is revealed by another angel, who declares that Babylon has fallen.

As we discussed in chapter 5 of this book, Babylon has always been identified as an adversary of the people of God. "Mystery Babylon" is not the ancient city on the Euphrates River, but the city of Jerusalem, as controlled by corrupt leaders of the Jews; whom Jesus called "hypocrites, blind guides, serpents, a generation of vipers,"and "children of the devil" (Matthew 23; John 8:44). The third angel brings a warning to anyone who worships the beast, his image, and receives his mark in his forehead or hand, because they would drink of the wine of the wrath of the Lamb.

Next, John sees a white cloud. And the one who sits on the cloud is like the Son of Man, who has a golden crown on His head and a sharp sickle in His hand. This should not be difficult to identify this as Jesus, who is the King of Kings coming on a cloud; just as He told Caiaphas, the high priest, "…Hereafter shall [you] see the Son of man sitting on the right hand of power, and coming in the clouds of heaven" (Matthew 26:64).

Now, the fourth angel declares, "Thrust in [your] sickle, and reap: for the time is come for [you] to reap; for the harvest of the earth is ripe" (Revelation 14:15). This word, translated "ripe" here, means "dried" or "withered." This is not a reference to a harvest of good ripe fruit; but that which has withered and dried, and has no value.

It reminds us of Jesus' conversation with the eleven disciples on the way to Gethsemane, where He says, "If a man abide not in me, he is cast forth as a branch, and is withered; and men gather them, and cast them into the fire, and they are burned" (John 15:6). Remember, this is a time of great persecution against the Church, by the Jewish leaders and the Romans.

Now, another angel comes out of the Temple in heaven, with another sharp sickle. He is followed by yet another angel, that comes from the altar and cries to the angel with the sharp sickle, to reap the clusters of grapes of the land that are fully ripe, and cast them into the winepress of the wrath of God (Revelation 14:19).

Notice that these grapes are "fully ripe"; that is, mature and ready to be harvested, but this is not "good fruit" to be eaten. It is the fullness of wickedness that is to be crushed. This is much like what we see in *Genesis 15:16*, where God is showing Abraham the future judgment his children would bring upon the Amorites, or the nations of Canaan.

That judgment would not come on them yet, but after four generations, because the "iniquity of the Amorites is not yet full." Here, the fruit has fully matured, and the time of judgment has come; and the result would be upon those living outside of the city (of Jerusalem); with a crushing so complete that their blood would flow even to the horses' bridles (Revelation 14:20).

This imagery of blood flowing as deep as up to the horses' bridles is seen in both Vespasian's army when they slaughtered thousands of Jews on the Sea of Galilee (that flows into the Jordan River), and when Placidus slew over fifteen thousand Jews at the Jordan River. Josephus comments, "one might then see the lake all bloody, and full of dead bodies," and "Jordan could not be passed over, by reason of the dead bodies that were in it"

(Josephus: *The Wars of the Jews,* book 3; chpt. 10; sect. 9, and book 4; chpt. 7; sect. 6). The river was so filled with blood, that it would appear to the Romans as they crossed the Jordan that it was a river of blood that reached to the horses' bridles.

Revelation 15 introduces seven angels, who are given seven bowls filled with the seven last plagues, or judgments against apostate Israel. The song of Moses and the song of the Lamb are sung by those in heaven, who have gotten victory over the beast; just as the children of Israel had gotten victory over Pharaoh and the Egyptians who sought to destroy them.

The angels with the bowls are dressed in pure white; signifying that this judgment is righteous; for that generation had denied and crucified Jesus and persecuted the Church. The forty years are almost finished; the end of the age has come, and Jerusalem and the Temple will be destroyed.

In the beginning of chapter 16, the first three angels pour out their bowls of judgment on the land. This judgment parallels God's plagues in Egypt. The first is injurious and hurtful sores on those who had the mark of the beast and who worshiped his image. *Exodus 9* speaks of the boils that afflicted the Egyptians under God's judgment. *Deuteronomy 28:27* warns of the boils of Egypt, with tumors and festering sores coming upon the Israelites, if they turn away from the Lord.

The second and third angels pour out a judgment that turns the waters of the sea and the rivers and fountains into blood. Again, this is much like what happened with Moses and Pharaoh.

When the fourth angel pours out his bowl on the sun, he receives power to burn men with fire. This is just the opposite of God's protection over His people. In the desert, the glory cloud protected Israel from the scorching heat of the sun. The psalmist tells us the Lord is our shade, and that the sun will not smite you by day (Psalms 121:5-6).

Isaiah also declares that the Redeemer of Israel will set the prisoners free, and "They shall not hunger nor thirst; neither shall the heat nor the sun smite them" (Isaiah 49:10). The protection of God is removed from apostate Israel, and they are experiencing the judgment of God by the Romans, who march through the land of Israel and burn all the Jewish quarters in every region of the land.

The pouring out of judgment by the fifth angel is upon the throne of the beast. Not only did the Jews bring continued persecution upon the Church, but the beast (Rome/Nero) also brought great trouble upon the Church. We have already discussed Caesar Nero's purpose to rid Rome of the Christians; resulting in a time of severe persecution, where tens of thousands were martyred in the most horrific ways. This included many of the early apostles, including Peter, Paul, and James. The seat or throne of Nero, the beast, is included in this judgment. And, as a result, his kingdom is filled with darkness.

Once again, the lights are going out of this kingdom that is ruled by this primary persecutor of the Church. Soon, Nero's madness would lead him to suicide, and Rome would be thrust into civil war. The Roman historian Tacitus gives us a glimpse of the chaos suffered by the Romans after Nero's death:

> "The whole city presented a frightful caricature of its normal self: fighting, and casualties at one point, baths and restaurants at another, here the spilling of blood and the liter of dead bodies, close by prostitutes and their like – all the vice associated with a life of idleness and pleasure, all the dreadful deeds typical of a pitiless sack. These were so intimately linked that an observer would have thought

Rome in the grip of a simultaneous orgy of violence and dissipation" (Tacitus, *The Histories*, book III; sect. 83).

Israel, as well as the beast, continually "blasphemed the God of heaven because of their pains and their sores, and repented not of their deeds" (Revelation 16:11).

With the bowl of the sixth angel, the waters of the Euphrates River were dried up; making way for the kings of the East. The drying up of the waters is a familiar scene we have witnessed many times in the Scriptures: the Red Sea, with Moses preserving the people of God from the Egyptian armies; and the Jordan River, with Joshua, as Israel crossed over to conquer their enemies in Canaan. Each signify the making of a passage for armies to cross in conquest.

Now the Roman battalions, along with the armies of the allied kings, are crossing the northeast boundary of Israel to invade and destroy apostate Israel. This is the same event we have seen in chapter 9 of *Revelation,* where again, the sixth angel is releasing the four "angels" that are bound in the Euphrates, and who will slay a third of the Jews.

John then sees three evil spirits that come out of the mouth of the dragon, the beast, and the false prophet. Both the beast of Rome and the false prophet of apostate Israel are in alliance with Satan, the dragon. These demonic powers go out to gather the kings of the earth and "the whole world" (Roman world), to the battle of the great day of God Almighty" (Revelation 16:16).

This is the day Jesus talked about when He would come "as a thief" (Matthew 24:43) – that is, unexpectedly, when not one stone would be left upon another; when the Temple and the city would be destroyed. This is the same event Jesus spoke of in *Matthew 24,* when He said that all these things would come upon "this generation" – those who were living during the forty years between A.D. 30 (Jesus' resurrection) and A.D. 70 (the destruction of the city and the Temple in *Matthew 24:34*).

The warning to both the Jews and the Church was to be watchful. If you knew when a thief was coming to break into your house; you would watch for him and guard your possessions. This would happen at an unexpected hour that no one would know about before the time. So, be watchful day and night. Jesus said this about two working in the field or two grinding at a mill: one would be taken and the other one left (Matthew 24:40-41). The warning was about an unexpected and sudden event that would require their watching for the fulfillment of the words of Jesus:

> Then let them which be in Judaea flee into the mountains: Let him which is on the housetop not come down to take anything out of his house: Neither let him which is in the field return back to take his clothes" (Matthew 24:16-18).

Jesus would come as a thief, and only those who are "watching" would be saved in the day of this great battle. Both Paul and Peter warned the churches.

> But ye, brethren, are not in darkness, that that day should overtake you as a thief (1 Thessalonians 5:4).

> But the day of the Lord will come as a thief in the night; in the which the heavens shall pass away with a great noise, and the elements shall melt with fervent heat, the earth also and the works that are therein shall be burned up (2 Peter 3:10).

We have already looked at the passing of the earth and heavens (destruction of a kingdom or an "age"), and the elements melting in a great conflagration when the Temple is destroyed (see chapter 4 of this book).

With the pouring out of the bowl of the sixth angel, the battle of the great day of God Almighty has come. This place of battle is identified as Armageddon or Har-Magedon, which is translated either as "city" or "mountain" of Megiddo. But Megiddo is neither a city nor a mountain. Rather, it is a valley where some of the greatest victories for Israel were fought – when they followed the Lord – and it was also a place of great slaughter when they had forsaken God.

It is identified as a place of great mourning; where the beloved King Josiah of Judah died, when he disobeyed the Word of God, by going out to fight the Egyptian King Necho (2 Chronicles 35:20-27). This defeat of Josiah became a symbol of great mourning for generations. A hundred years later, the prophet Zechariah used this event to describe great mourning, when:

> …the inhabitants of Jerusalem…shall look upon me whom they have pierced, and they shall mourn for him, as one [mourns] for his only son…In that day shall there be a great mourning in Jerusalem, as the mourning of Hadadrimmon in the valley of Megiddon (Zechariah 12:10-11).

Hadadrimmon is a place in the valley of Megiddo where they held a national lamentation for the death of King Josiah. So, Armageddon is identified as a place of great slaughter and mourning for apostate Israel, when God's wrath was poured out upon them by the Romans.

This "great city" is remembered by God as "Babylon" (a symbolic name for Israel and Jerusalem, as we have already discussed), who receives the "fierceness of his wrath" (Revelation 16:19). Verse 18 mentions a "great earthquake" that divides the city into three parts. This earthquake is probably symbolic for a great shaking, as is described in *Hebrews*, which says:

Yet once more I shake not the earth only, but also heaven. And this word, Yet once more, [signifies] the removing of those things that are shaken, as of things that are made, that those things which cannot be shaken may remain. Wherefore we receiving a kingdom which cannot be moved (Hebrews 12:26-28).

The end of the age has come, and the stone Temple built by man, and the old system of sacrifice is shaken to the ground. Although I believe that this earthquake is symbolic; it is interesting that the Jewish historian Josephus told of violent storms and an earthquake in the time of the destruction of Jerusalem:

"…for there broke out a prodigious storm in the night, with the utmost violence, and very strong winds, with the largest showers of rain, with continual lightnings, terrible thunderings, and amazing concussions and bellowings of the earth, that was in an earthquake. These things were a manifest indication that some destruction was coming upon men, when the system of the world was put into this disorder; and anyone would guess that these wonders foreshowed some grand calamities that were coming" (Josephus: *The Wars of the Jews*, book 4; chpt. 4; sect. 5).

The last verse of this chapter speaks of "And great hail from heaven fell upon men, each hailstone about the weight of a talent." The Romans hurled cannonball-like stones from their catapults against the walls and into the city of Jerusalem, causing great damage. Again, I refer to Josephus and his description of the damage caused by these catapults:

"Now, the stones that were cast, were of the weight of a talent, and were carried two furlongs and farther. The blow they gave was no way to be sustained, not only by those that stood first in the way, but by those that were beyond them for a great space. As for the Jews, they at first watched the coming of the stone, for it was of a white color, and could therefore not only be perceived by the great noise it made, but could be seen also before it came by its brightness; accordingly the watchmen that sat upon the towers gave them notice when the engine was let go, and the stone came from it, and cried out aloud in their own country language, "THE SON COMETH" so those that were in its way stood off, and threw themselves down upon the ground; by which means, and by their thus guarding themselves, the stone fell down and did them no harm. But the Romans contrived how to prevent that by blacking the stone, who then could aim at them with success, when the stone was not discerned beforehand, as it had been till then; and so they destroyed many of them at one blow." (Josephus: *The Wars of the Jews*, book 5; chpt. 6; sect. 3).

This hail of great stones, each weighing about a talent, parallel's this "plague" that was "exceedingly great" (Revelation 16:21).

Chapter 12

The Great Whore and the Scarlet-Colored Beast

REVELATION *17* OPENS WITH AN angel that had one of the seven bowls, which came to John to show him "the great whore that sits upon many waters." John is carried away in the spirit, to a wilderness where he sees a woman. Upon her forehead, a name is written, "MYSTERY, BABYLON THE GREAT, THE MOTHER OF HARLOTS AND ABOMINATIONS OF THE EARTH." She is riding a scarlet-colored beast, with seven heads and ten horns. We have already looked at this portion of Scripture in chapter 5 of this book.

This Harlot contrasts with the Bride; and the Harlot is in league with the Romans, to bring persecution against Jesus, and then the Church.

The high priest and the Jewish leaders arrested Jesus and brought Him to Pilate, to have him crucified. Pilate recognized that the reason behind their accusations against Jesus was envy. He wanted to release Jesus. But the crowd of Jewish leaders prevailed after threatening him, that if he released a man who identified himself as a king instead of Caesar, then he would be in trouble with his superiors. Pilate conceded and Jesus was crucified.

Then the Jews determined to destroy the followers of Jesus, just as Jesus said it would happen. "Wherefore, behold, I send unto you prophets, and wise men, and scribes: and some of them [you] shall kill and crucify; and some of them shall [you] scourge in your synagogues, and persecute them from city to city" (Matthew 23:34).

Over and over, we see the Jewish leaders instigating Roman leaders to bring persecution against the Church. Herod slew James, the brother of John with a sword; and because it pleased the Jews, he arrested Peter and purposed to execute him the next day (Acts 12:1-4).

Are the spiritual leaders of Israel identified by John as Babylon, the great the mother of harlots? Isaiah prophesied of Jerusalem's future harlotry in his day, "How the faithful city has become a harlot! It was full of justice; Righteousness lodged in it, But now murderers" (Isaiah 1:21 NKJV).

Now, in John's day, Israel has rejected the new covenant and sided with Rome (the scarlet-colored beast with seven heads and ten horns). Beginning with verse seven, the angel who comes to John begins to explain the mystery of the woman and the beast to him. We have already identified the beast as the Roman Empire, and Nero, who was also referred to as the beast. Here, the seven heads of the beast are identified as seven mountains or hills, upon which the woman sits.

Historically, the city of Rome is identified as "the city of seven hills." Not only do the seven hills represent the city of Rome; but here, the angel explains that associated with this city are seven kings, and "…five are fallen, and one is, and the other is not yet come; and when he [comes], he must continue a short space" (Revelation 17:10).

The Great Whore and the Scarlet-Colored Beast

If we look at first century historians such as Suetonius and Josephus; they identify the Roman Emperors as: Julius Caesar, Augustus Caesar, Tiberias Caesar, Caligula, Claudius, and Nero. Galba, Otho, and Vitellius each declared themselves "Emperor" after the death of Nero, but each of them only survived a few months.

At the time of the writing of *Revelation*, the first five emperors have fallen. The one that "is," is Nero, who is the sixth. The other that is "not yet come" is Galba, who truly was Emperor for "a short space" (June AD 68 to January AD 69).

The players described in chapter 17 are the beast; with its seven heads and ten horns, "that was, and is not, and yet is, and has ascended out of the bottomless pit and goes into perdition (ruin, loss, destruction); and the woman; the seven mountains; seven kings; and ten kings with no kingdom. All of these make war with the Lamb, but the Lamb will overcome them.

Trying to identify all of these symbolic characters is challenging, but if we keep in mind the confederacy between Rome, the apostate Jewish leaders, and the beast that ascends out of the bottomless pit (the dragon or the devil), we can see that the purpose of this alliance is to war with the Lamb (Jesus).

We have already seen how the Jewish leaders rejected Jesus and used the Roman authorities to try and destroy the Church. The height of this persecution was under Nero, the sixth Emperor of Rome. But the real manipulator from the pit (abyss) is Satan, who always brings ruin and death. With Nero's intense persecution against the Church, many believers and Church leaders died during those three and one-half years. But in the end, havoc and destruction came against both Rome and the Jews, and which ended in the destruction of Jerusalem and the Temple.

Nero declared war on the Jews, but then committed suicide; which threw Rome into a major civil war. Rival Roman generals marched with their armies to conquer Rome and secure the Empire for themselves. A quick succession of self-declared emperors, which ended with their assassinations, was known as "the year of the four emperors." The Empire appeared to be doomed, until Vespasian conquered Rome and was able to maintain law and order and restore the city of Rome and all ten provinces of the empire under his control. It seemed that the head of the beast had been wounded to death, but its deadly wound was, in fact, healed.

While Vespasian was occupied with securing the Empire, his son Titus was gathering troops from the Roman provinces and besieging the city of Jerusalem. Within five months, the Romans destroyed the city from without; even as Jewish militant factions were destroying one another from within. In A.D. 70, the city fell and the Temple was destroyed.

The multiple kings in alliance with the Romans helped destroy the Jews and the city of Jerusalem. God had "put in their hearts to fulfill his will, and to agree, and give their kingdom unto the beast." The result of their hatred of Israel caused them to "make her desolate and naked, and ...eat her flesh, and burn her with fire" (Revelation 17:16-17).

The woman is identified as "that great city," which reigned over the kings of the earth. This same term is used in *Revelation 11:8*. "And their dead bodies shall lie in the street of the great city, which spiritually is called Sodom, and Egypt, where also our Lord was crucified." Jerusalem was often referred to as a harlot; chasing her lovers and forsaking the Lord (see Jeremiah 2:2,20; 3:1-3,6,14,20).

The Great Whore and the Scarlet-Colored Beast

Chapter eighteen continues with the theme of Jerusalem's destruction. A strong angel comes down from heaven to announce that Babylon the great is fallen. In describing the city, he says it "has become a dwelling place of demons, a prison for every foul spirit, and the cage of every unclean and hated bird!" (Revelation 18:2 NKJV). The chapter continues to describe the end of this city as with plagues, death, mourning, and famine. It shall be utterly burned with fire and with great violence shall it be thrown down (Revelation 18:4,8,21). A similar description is given about the ancient city of Babylon, and of Edom after God's judgment.

> Its smoke shall ascend forever. From generation to generation it shall lie waste…the pelican and the porcupine shall possess it, Also the owl and the raven shall dwell in it…And thorns shall come up in its palaces, Nettles, and brambles in its fortresses; It shall be a habitation of jackals, A courtyard for ostriches…night creatures shall rest there (Isaiah 34:10-14 NKJV).

> But wild beasts of the desert will lie there, And their houses will be full of owls; Ostriches will dwell there, And wild goats…hyenas…and jackals (Isaiah 13:21-22 NKJV).

Some writers have identified "Babylon the Great" as the ancient city of Babylon on the Euphrates River; but this could not be, for ancient Babylon became a city of no significance and continual decline, after it was conquered by Alexander the Great in 331 B.C. Symbolically, the term "Babylon" has always been identified with rebellion against God, and oppression and persecution against the people of God. Jerusalem, the city of the Great King and the dwelling place of God, has now become Babylon; known for its sorcery and wickedness.

This vast destruction causes kings, merchants, and shipmasters to weep when they see Jerusalem and the Temple destroyed. Their grieving was because of the financial loss they would experience. The wealth controlled by the chief priests was immense. The fine linen, purple, and scarlet; gold, precious stones, pearls, and great riches were all to be destroyed. The reason for this devastation was because "in her was found the blood of prophets and saints, and of all who were slain on the earth" (Revelation 18:24 NKJV).

Again, this reminds us of the words of Jesus, concerning the religious leaders in Jerusalem, "That upon you may come all the righteous blood shed upon the earth" (Matthew 23:35).

In verse 21, the mighty angel takes up a millstone and casts it into the sea; which describes the extreme violence that causes this city to be thrown down. Throwing a milestone into the sea reminds us of the words of Jesus, as He describes those who bring offences, "It were better for him that a millstone were hanged about his neck, and he cast into the sea, than that he should offend one of these little ones" (Luke 17:2).

"Little ones" here is not only in reference to children, but also to the "least" or to those "less in rank or influence." The city of Jerusalem was a type of Babylon that caused many to sin. The religious leaders enticed believers to blaspheme; and attempted to draw people away from the faith. The Apostle Paul himself said he "…punished them oft in every synagogue, and compelled them to blaspheme; and being exceedingly mad against them, I persecuted them even unto strange cities" (Acts 26:11).

Paul's testimony of how he persecuted believers, as a leader of the Pharisees before his conversion, describes how the religious leaders in Jerusalem were attempting to destroy the Church. The many offences of the city of Jerusalem, would bring upon them, the violence described as a millstone being cast into the sea.

The remainder of chapter eighteen describes the city after these judgments are completed. No more will there be musicians, craftsmen, the light of a candle, the sound of the millstone, or the voices of a bride or a bridegroom. This description parallels God's judgment on the land as described by the prophets Isaiah and Jeremiah:

> ...the mirth of tabrets [ceases], the noise of them that rejoice [is ended] ...the city of confusion is broken down...all joy is darkened, the mirth of the land is gone (Isaiah 24:1-12).

> ...I will take from them the voice of mirth, and the voice of gladness, the voice of the bridegroom, and the voice of the bride, the sound of the millstones, and the light of the candle. And this whole land shall be a desolation (Jeremiah 25:10-11).

Revelation 19 takes us to a heavenly perspective, regarding the judgment of the harlot system that was in league with the kings of the earth. The sound of great praise fills heaven, as the voices of a great multitude are praising God for the righteous judgments upon spiritual Babylon, "which did corrupt the earth with her fornication..." (Revelation 19:2).

The Temple, housed in the city of Jerusalem, was the center of the old covenant worship, with its priests and sacrificial system. This was a legitimate operation waiting for the Messiah to come. But now the Messiah had come; instead of embracing the fulfillment of the many promises God had given of a new covenant, the Temple rulers rejected the Messiah and persecuted those He had sent.

They were as the vinedressers in the parable Jesus told of the coming kingdom of God (Matthew 21:33-46). In the parable, the owner leased the vineyard to vinedressers, who were to care for the vineyard and give the owner its fruit. When the fruit had ripened, the owner sent his servants to receive the fruit. The vinedressers refused; and beat some and killed some of those that the owner had sent to them.

The owner then sent his son to receive the fruit on his behalf, but when they saw him, they said, "This is the heir; come, let us kill him, and let us seize on his inheritance" (verse 38). They wanted the vineyard for themselves. As a result of their defiance, they were destroyed and the vineyard was given to others.

This parable describes the harlotry of the leaders in charge of the Temple, with its system of sacrifices and the great wealth it produced. The new covenant had no need of a stone Temple or animal sacrifices. The blood of Jesus was the only and forever sacrifice God would except on man's behalf, and the new Temple was the believers themselves.

> "But Christ, being a high priest of good things to come, by a greater and more perfect tabernacle, not made with hands; that is to say, not of this building" (Hebrews 9:11 PARAPHRASED)

> "For Christ is not entered into the holy places made with hands, which are the figures of the true; but into heaven itself, now to appear in the presence of God for us" (Hebrews 9:24).

Along with the "Alleluias" of the heavenly multitudes, is the declaration that "her smoke rises up for ever and ever" (Revelation 19:3). The smoke rising from the burned city and Temple is not eternal; but the end of the old covenant system is. There will never again be a need for a man-made Temple.

The Great Whore and the Scarlet-Colored Beast

Revelation 19:4-9 reveal the praises of the multitudes in heaven, as it is declared that "the Lord God Omnipotent reigns… for the marriage of the Lamb has come." Weddings and marriages in Scripture are in reference to a great feast; a celebration of the bride and groom.

What does a wedding feast have to do with the destruction of the city of Jerusalem and the Temple? There is a theme that runs throughout the Scriptures, from *Genesis* to *Revelation*. This theme concerns the dwelling place of God and His people. In *Genesis*, God created a place for man in His presence, in the Garden of Eden. When man sinned, he was put out of the garden, or from the presence of God. The next four books (*Exodus-Deuteronomy*) were about creating the Tabernacle; a dwelling place for God, in the midst of His people.

From the Tabernacle of Moses to the tent of David; and to the Temple of Solomon and the rebuilt Temple after the exile, God's dwelling place was to be among the people of Israel, but the stone Temples that were built were only earthly models (Hebrews 8:2; 9:11). The man-made Temple and its system of sacrifices was replaced with the new covenant Temple, where God lives "within" the believer (Hebrews 8:6-13; 1 Corinthians 3:16; 6:19; Ephesians 2:19-22).

This spiritual Temple God inhabits can now happen because the veil of sin that separated God and man was torn at the cross, and our access to God's presence was made possible.

There are many examples given to us in the New Testament, to show our relationship with God. We are called the Temple of God, built on the foundation of Jesus Christ (1 Corinthians 3:11). We are the Church of God that Jesus is building on the revelation that He "is the Christ, the Son of the living God" (Matthew 16:16-18).

We are a city made up of individual, precious stones that are being fitted together for a dwelling place of God (Ephesians 2:22). We are the "wife," the "bride of Christ," as those brought into the family of God to share in His life, position, and inheritance (Ephesians 2:6; 3:15; Romans 8:14-17; Revelation 19:7-9; 21:9).

The marriage theme continues in chapter 21; identifying the "bride" as the city named "New Jerusalem." Again, this city is built with individual, living stones (believers) that make up this spiritual city. It has no Temple in it, for "the Lord God Almighty and the Lamb are the temple" (Revelation 21:10,22). God dwelling with His people becomes an eternal reality!

As we return to chapter nineteen, we see heaven opened, to reveal a rider on a white horse, and followed by armies on white horses. The identity of this rider is revealed as one called "Faithful and True," and His name is "The Word of God" and "KING OF KINGS, AND LORD OF LORDS," whose eyes are as a flame of fire (Revelation 19:11-16).

The rider is, of course, the Lord Jesus, who is described in chapter one with eyes as a flame of fire, and with a two-edged sword coming out of His mouth. We know the Word of God is sharper than any two-edged sword (Hebrews 4:12) and it is the Word of God "who is God," and who "became flesh and dwelt among us" (John 1:1,14).

This rider has a name "that no man knew, but he himself" (Revelation 19:12). This name, however, is not a secret that no one knows, for His name is revealed to us; but the meaning here is that He is the only one who owns this name. He alone is KING OF KINGS AND LORD OF LORDS.

The imagery here shows the Word of God going forth throughout the whole earth, and conquering the nations; not by military force, but by the prophetic Word of God and the armies of believers who declare it.

Some would point out that these "armies" are in heaven, not on the earth; but we need to remember that from God's perspective, there is no difference. He "raised us up together, (with him) and made us sit together in heavenly places in Christ Jesus" (Ephesians 2:6). This is not when we leave earth and go to heaven, but when we are born-again.

When the Word of God marched into our lives and revealed to us the Lordship of Jesus; the Word of God conquered us, and we believed in our hearts and were made new creations (Colossians 1:5,6; Romans 10:8,9; 2 Corinthians 5:17). Our residence may be on the earth, but our citizenship is in heaven. Jesus said that when believers receive the power of the Holy Spirit, they will be witnesses for Him first in Jerusalem, then in Judea, and Samaria, and unto the uttermost parts of the earth (Acts 1:8).

The armies of believers have been advancing throughout the whole earth, ever since the resurrection and ascension of Jesus. And they will continue to do so until all His enemies have been put beneath His feet. "His kingdom is an everlasting kingdom," and "of the increase of his government and peace there shall be no end" (Daniel 4:3; Isaiah 9:7).

These aspects of the kingdom of God advancing throughout the earth will continue until Jesus returns, but now our focus returns to the prophetic Word concerning apostate Israel and the beast of Rome.

The rider of the white horse has "a vesture dipped in blood." We know that our redemption is because of the shed blood of Jesus, and that could be referenced here, but most likely it is the blood of His enemies, as He (the Word of God) has "[tread] the winepress of the fierceness and wrath of Almighty God" (Revelation 19:15).

Jesus' prophetic Word regarding the destruction of the Temple and the city of Jerusalem shows that the city will be "trampled underfoot by the Gentiles" (Luke 21:24 PARAPHRASED). The angel, standing in the sun or in the light of day, calls to the birds of the air to come to a great feast, where they will eat the flesh of kings, captains, mighty men, and horses. They are filled with the flesh of the slain; killed by the swords of those fulfilling the Word of God for Jesus, who said, "this generation shall not pass, till all these things be fulfilled" (Matthew 24:34).

The beast and his armies "gathered together to make war against him that sat on the horse, and against his army" (Revelation 19:19). Both the beast of Rome and the false prophet (apostate Israel) brought severe persecution against the Lord Jesus and the Church; but now they are "cast alive into a lake of fire burning with brimstone" (Revelation 19:20).

Fire and brimstone speak of judgment, such as fell on the cities of Sodom and Gomorrah in Abraham's day. Nero, the beast of Rome, and apostate Israel (the false prophet) are cast into the place of judgment. Both were persecutors standing in opposition against God; but during this time of judgment, Nero commits suicide, and throws the empire into civil war. What follows is the systematic annihilation of the Jews in Jerusalem, and most every city of the empire is brought into a time of great tribulation. In the end, the birds of the air feasted on the many bodies of the slain.

Chapter 13

Satan is Bound, Loosed, and Destroyed

A New Heaven, a New Earth, a New Age

Much of the *Book of Revelation* is about the events that John saw in a series of visions while exiled on the isle of Patmos. Most of those events took place during those forty years between the resurrection of Jesus and the destruction of the city of Jerusalem and the Temple, in A.D. 70. The *Book of Revelation* begins with a message to John about "things which must shortly come to pass...for the time is at hand" (Revelation 1:1,3).

Again, at the very end of the book, John was told, "...the things which must shortly be done...behold, I come quickly..." (Revelation 22:6,20 paraphrased). John is also told to write of things, "which [you have] seen, and the things which are, and the things which shall be hereafter" (Revelation 1:19). It seems that chapters 1-19 are regarding the events John "has seen and are"; and chapters 20-22 concern the things "which shall be hereafter."

We have already discussed the symbols and their meanings found in *Revelation* chapters 20-22, in chapter 4 of this book. So, instead of rehearsing these things again, I recommend for you to go back and reread chapter 4.

Revelation 20 describes the work of Jesus, to bind and destroy the devil. Jesus, the strong angel, comes from heaven with the key (authority) and binds the devil; casting him into a "bottomless pit," and sealing him up (limiting his activity) from deceiving the nations for a long period of time (a thousand years). After this long time, Satan will be loosed for a short season (Revelation 20:1-3). He is loosed to gather the nations described as Gog and Magog, whose armies surround the beloved city (New Jerusalem), to destroy it, but God sends a fire from heaven that devours them and the devil is cast into the lake of fire (Revelation 20:7-10).

The language is spiritual and symbolic. Jesus did not bind a spiritual entity with a physical chain. The devil's binding is accomplished with words of spiritual authority. Jesus declared, "All authority is given unto me in heaven and in earth." He then told His disciples (which includes all of us) to go to all the world and proclaim the gospel and make disciples of all nations (Matthew 28:18-20).

We can see the people of all nations respond to the gospel and enter the kingdom of God, because the devil that deceived them and blinded their minds from the knowledge of the truth, has been bound by Jesus; who then gives us the same authority (2 Corinthians 4:3-4; Matthew 18:18-19).

The authority to bind the devil is given to all the Church. Jesus says, "Verily I say unto you, whatsoever [you] shall bind on earth shall be bound in heaven: and whatsoever [you] shall loose on earth shall be loosed in heaven" (Matthew 18:18).

This truth is more clearly stated in the *Amplified* translation, which indicates that the Church has been given the authority to enforce on earth, what has been done in heaven. Whatever you forbid and declare to be improper and unlawful on earth, *must* be what is already forbidden in heaven. Words bind the devil. Words either allow or disallow his activity and that of his kingdom. Jesus bound the devil with words that chained him, and Jesus gives us the same authority.

With the elimination of Satan and everything that is not in the Lamb's book of life, the earth and the heavens are cleansed. All opposition to the kingdom of God (righteousness, peace, and joy), and everything that defiles and brings fear, sorrow, and pain are cast into the lake of fire (Revelation 21:4,8,27).

Chapter twenty-one describes the Bride, the Lamb's wife. When John looks to see the bride, he sees instead, a city named New Jerusalem, descending from heaven and having the glory of God. The dimensions of the city are noted, and its building materials show that it is made of the most precious and beautiful gemstones. These stones are alive and are fitly joined together, to make a spiritual building inhabited by the Lord, who is the very Temple Himself.

The last chapter of *Revelation* reveals the source of a pure river of the water of life; it flows from the throne of God and of the Lamb. This is the same river we see in Ezekiel's vision (Ezekiel 47:1-12). Ezekiel saw the waters issue forth from the threshold of the Temple; and flow toward the east, across the desert, and into the Dead Sea. These living waters brought life to everything they touched; even causing the waters of the Dead Sea to come alive and contain a multitude of fish. Ezekiel also saw many trees on either side of the river bearing an abundance of fruit, just as John saw.

This river should be familiar to us; reminding us of the river that flowed through and watered the Garden of Eden. John also writes in the *Gospel of John*, the words of Jesus:

> If any man thirst, let him come unto me, and drink. He that [believes] on me as the scripture [has] said, out of his belly shall flow rivers of living water. (But this [spoke] he of the Spirit, which they that believe on him should receive: for the Holy Ghost was not yet given; because that Jesus was not yet glorified.) (John 7:37-39).

This spiritual river is the Holy Spirit, who lives in every believer; and every believer is the Temple of God. What flows from us (our lives) should bring forth good fruit and healing for all to partake of, that are around us.

John tells us that in this city, there is "no night there." It is the light of God's glory that enlightens this city, for "God is light, and in him is no darkness at all" (1 John 1:5). The city is made up of all of the redeemed of all ages. And no more will there be in it, a curse to bring pain, sadness, or disappointment, because the source of all of those things (sin) is removed forever.

John concludes this book with a reminder that the things that were revealed to him "must shortly be done"; and Jesus declares, "Behold, I come quickly" (Revelation 22:6-7).

Chapter 14

The Nature of Judgment

In *Mathew 24,* we see the warning of great judgment upon Jerusalem, the cities that opposed Jesus, and those who rejected the ones Jesus sent to them. In the *Book of Revelation,* we see that work of judgment being carried out. What we may not understand is why judgment came upon these cities.

Many may read the accounts of the terrible suffering and pain this judgment brought, and be led to believe that it was because of God's hatred of those who rejected and crucified His Son. But we need to take a closer look at the Scriptures to understand the nature, cause, and purpose of judgment.

What is judgment?

According to *The Strong's Concordance*, the definition of the word "judgment" is as follows: (Strong's [G2917] *krima*, a decision (the function or the effect, for or against ("crime").

Therefore, we could say that biblical judgment is a decision that functions to bring about an effect for a crime. A crime is anything that is illegal; that which violates a law. The Bible is full of laws against sin. "Sin is the transgression of the law" (1 John 3:4).

Why is God so serious about sin? It is because the "wages [results] of sin is death" (Romans 6:23). In God's kingdom, there is no death, no pain, no sadness, and no sickness. Guilt, shame, oppression, and fear are not allowed in the kingdom of God; and all of these things are the result of sin. God's hatred of sin is an expression of His love for people, to protect us from the evil consequences of sin.

When God created man, He gave him dominion and the commandment to "be fruitful and to multiply." God wanted man to increase and abound, and enjoy everything God had given him.

In the first several chapters of the *Book of Genesis*, we have the story of Adam and Eve; and their disobedience to God's Word and the resulting death that their actions produced. No, they did not die physically the day that they sinned, but death was the result. Death is not a "ceasing to exist," but a separation from God. The day they sinned, they experienced a spiritual death. Since God is the source of all life and blessing; being separated from Him took them to a place outside of God's presence and into an environment of shame and guilt and death – first spiritually and eventually, physically.

It was their disobedience that brought about the judgment for sin. Some may blame the devil for tempting them. Others may even blame God for giving man the power of choice. But the heartbreak of their fallen condition was the result of their sin, that initiated the judgment God had warned them about.

Who is the judge?

The Nature of Judgment

Jesus explains the work of judgment. "For the Father [judges] no man, but [has] committed all judgment unto the Son" (John 5:22). The Bible tells us that God, the Father, has committed all judgment to the Son (Jesus). And Jesus tells us that He has come to judge no one, but has committed all judgment to the Word of God (John 12:46-48). So, the Word of God is the standard of righteousness that will bring about a judgment when it is violated. Judgment is not to punish man but to destroy the results of sin.

What does it mean to commit all judgment to the Word of God?

God's Word is the unchangeable expression of the will of God. John describes the Word of God to us:

> In the beginning was the Word, and the Word was with God, and the Word was God. The same was in the beginning with God. All things were made by him (the Word); and without him was not anything made that was made (John 1:1-3).

In the first chapter of *Genesis,* God spoke and His words produced all of creation. Again, in *Psalms 33:6,9* , we see that "By the word of the LORD were the heavens made; and all the host of them by the breath of his mouth… For he [spoke], and it was done; he commanded, and it stood fast." This Word … "became flesh and dwelt among us" (John 1:14 CSB).

By His words and deeds, Jesus was the perfect expression of God (Hebrews 1:1-3). The Word of God is "forever…settled in heaven" (Psalms 119:89). God's Word is eternal, and what He has spoken will surely come to pass; it will not return to Him empty or void, but will accomplish what He has spoken (Isaiah 55:11).

That is why God told Moses to write down His words and teach them to the nation of Israel; because it would protect them from the consequences of sin (disobedience). "…I have set before you life and death, blessing and cursing: therefore choose life, that both [you] and [your] seed may live" (Deuteronomy 30:19).

Many times throughout the Scriptures, we see man's sinfulness and the impending judgment that results. We also see God's desire to preserve man from judgment, by sending prophets to the people before judgment came. If the people will hear God's Word by the prophet and "repent," that is "change their thinking" and turn to God, then forgiveness is given and judgment is diverted.

A good example of this is when God sent the prophet Jonah to the city of Nineveh with the message that judgment would fall on them in forty days, unless they would repent. You might remember that Jonah ran from his assignment because he wanted judgment to fall on the people of that city. Nineveh was a capital city of the Assyrian Empire, and their armies had invaded Israel, where Jonah lived. They were his enemies, and he wanted them to be destroyed, but God wanted to preserve them and keep them from experiencing that judgment.

God prepared a fish to swallow Jonah; not just to save Jonah, but to save Nineveh. Here we see the heart of God. The spiritual truth is that sin will bring judgment, and God does not take any delight in judgment because judgment brings death and destruction – and those things are not a part of God's kingdom. When Jonah reluctantly went and preached to the Ninevites, they did repent and were saved from judgment.

The Nature of Judgment

Even when Israel's enemies were destroyed because of sin, God was more than just saddened. When judgment fell on Moab; it says of God, "Therefore will I howl for Moab, and I will cry out for all Moab; mine heart shall mourn for the men of Kirheres" (Jeremiah 48:31). We see God howls, or wails in sorrow for the destruction that came upon the people of Moab.

When Judah and the people of Jerusalem were about to be destroyed for their wickedness, God sought for someone to intercede on behalf of the people.

> And I sought for a man among them, that should make up the hedge, and stand in the gap before me for the land, that I should not destroy it: but I found none. Therefore, have I poured out mine indignation upon them; I have consumed them with the fire of my wrath: their own way have I recompensed upon their heads, saith the LORD GOD (Ezekiel 22:30-31).

God takes no pleasure in anyone's destruction, and He attempts to divert judgment from coming; but in this case, there was no one to bring a word of repentance to the people, so judgment fell. Now the same scenario is being played out over Jerusalem in Jesus' day.

> O Jerusalem, Jerusalem, the one who kills the prophets and stones those who are sent to her! How often I wanted to gather your children together, as a hen gathers her chicks under *her* wings, but you were not willing! See! Your house is left to you desolate (Matthew 23:36-38 NKJV).

Jesus mourned over Jerusalem and the judgment that was to come upon them. In His words to the scribes and Pharisees were eight "woes." This word "woe" is a primary exclamation of grief. Jesus is not happily pronouncing judgment on these religious leaders or the people of Jerusalem for rejecting Him. Instead, He is grieving over their coming destruction.

Wherever there is sin, there must be judgment. The purpose of judgment is to eradicate sin and the accompanying fear and pain it brings.

> *There is* therefore now no condemnation to those who are in Christ Jesus, who walk not according to the flesh, but according to the Spirit. For the law of the Spirit of life in Christ Jesus has made me free from the law of sin and death (Romans 8:1-2).

The law of sin and death is simply stated as, "if you sin, there is a judgment required for that sin, and that judgment is death." The eighth chapter of *Romans* is all about mankind's inability to keep the Law of God. Therefore, God sent His own Son in the flesh to perfectly keep the Law of God for us.

Jesus also received the required judgment for man's sin so that we could be declared righteous before God – not with our own righteousness because of our works, but with His righteousness, which we receive by faith. Jesus was condemned, judged, and punished for our sin, to remove from us, the judgment that the Law of God required.

So, if Jesus received the judgment for all of the sins of all humanity, then why is there still sin and judgment today? Why did God bring such harsh judgment on the Jews and the city of Jerusalem in A.D. 70?

Let's consider this question from both a legal and a practical point of view. Legally, the sins of all humanity were paid for on the cross when Jesus received the righteous judgment that God's Law required for sin. A question we need to answer is, "Did the

The Nature of Judgment

sacrifice of Jesus on the cross overturn the law of sin and death? Is death and all of its auxiliary works still a result of sin today?

I believe that answer is right here in *Romans 8*.

> ...that the righteous requirement of the law might be fulfilled in us who do not walk according to the flesh but according to the Spirit. For those who live according to the flesh set their minds on the things of the flesh, but those *who live* according to the Spirit, the things of the Spirit. For to be carnally minded *is* death, but to be spiritually minded *is* life and peace. Because the carnal mind *is* enmity against God; for it is not subject to the law of God, nor indeed can be. So then, those who are in the flesh cannot please God. But you are not in the flesh but in the Spirit, if indeed the Spirit of God dwells in you. Now if anyone does not have the Spirit of Christ, he is not His. And if Christ *is* in you, the body *is* dead because of sin, but the Spirit *is* life because of righteousness" (Romans 8:4-10 NKJV).

Legally, the price has been paid for all humanity to be forgiven and freed from the judgment that sin requires. Practically speaking, keeping the Law of God is still impossible because of the "weakness of the flesh" (Romans 8:3). To be "carnally minded" is to form opinions and come to conclusions based on your physical surroundings and senses.

If I live according to how something appears to be or how I feel, I am allowing my body and my mind to govern my actions. If I am yielding my body to do the will of God and I am renewing my mind to think according to what God's Word says (Romans 12:1-2), then I am being spiritually-minded and am led by the Spirit of God which brings me life and peace (Romans 8:5-6,14).

I believe that one of the greatest revelations a Christian can receive is to understand that they are a three-part being – spirit, soul, and body (1 Thessalonians 5:23). When we come to faith in Jesus and are born-again, the part of us that is changed and "made righteous" is our spirit. We are made "a new creation" in Christ Jesus (2 Corinthians 5:17). We still live in the same flesh body and we still have the same mind. The body needs to be yielded to God, and the mind renewed to think differently.

We have the ability to follow the Spirit of God, who lives in us and wants to guide us; but we also have the ability to continue to follow our same unrenewed mind and the desires of the flesh. The outcome of our actions is either life or death (Romans 8:6).

We have probably all known someone who was born-again and who loved Jesus, but was bound with an addiction, such as drugs, alcoholism, or some other kind of destructive activity, that eventually destroyed their lives. Their marriage, career, ministry, or God-planned destiny for them was never fulfilled because their life ended tragically. Even though they were born-again and received, by faith, the righteousness of God and are forgiven and given eternal life; the judgment on sin still produced death.

"Do you not know that if you present yourselves to anyone as obedient slaves, you are slaves of the one whom you obey, either of sin, which leads to death, or of obedience, which leads to righteousness?" (Romans 6:16 ESV). We are righteous because of the work of Jesus, but we can have unrighteous works which still produce death, because it is a spiritual law.

Jesus wept over Jerusalem and the coming judgment upon that generation. He knew the price He was about to pay for their forgiveness, but He prophetically looked ahead and saw the judgment they would undergo. This nation had killed the prophets of old and would kill those Jesus would send to them. He foretold

The Nature of Judgment

of the fast-approaching judgment, and saw the awful destruction their sin and rejection would bring upon them.

Without repentance, their "house will be desolate," for the Word of God declared by Jesus would be fulfilled. They were not destroyed because of God's hatred for them, for Jesus said on the cross, "Father, forgive them, for they don't know what they are doing" (Luke 23:34 NET). God did not hate them, but mourned over their rejection of Jesus. The one God sent to rescue them was rejected, and their act of rejection is what brought upon them, great ruin.

Chapter 15

The Summary

THE BIRTH OF JESUS CHRIST of Nazareth fulfilled all of the prophetic words given to man of the coming Messiah and Savior. He was the Seed of the woman, the offspring of the seed of David, and He was Emmanuel, the one birthed by a virgin. He was the Branch and the Prophet; the messenger of the covenant; the Lion of the tribe of Judah, and the Lamb who was slain before the foundation of the world.

Jesus lived for 33½ years. He taught the multitudes and healed their sick. He set free the possessed and oppressed. He was the light that shinned in the darkness. He spoke with absolute authority and commanded the wind and waves to obey Him, and they did. He challenged the religious leaders with truth because they so grossly misrepresented God His Father. Jesus warned that generation of a time of terrible tribulation that would soon come upon them and that would result in the destruction of the city of Jerusalem and the Temple.

Jesus spoke of His coming kingdom and the glory of it, that would fill all the earth. He spoke of building His Church that the gates of hell would not prevail against. He taught His disciples to carry the gospel of the kingdom of God to all people in all nations; and the same works that He did, they would do, because the same Holy Spirit would anoint them with power.

Jesus rebuked the Pharisees and Sadducees, the doctors of the law, and the chief rulers at the Temple; warning them that they would see His coming in judgment upon that generation.

When Jesus died on the cross, His sacrifice for man's redemption was complete. Being resurrected from the dead; He defeated death, hell, and the grave. He destroyed the works of the devil; binding him from deceiving the nations, and making available eternal life to all who would believe.

After instructing His disciples, He ascended into heaven, where He was enthroned as King of the Everlasting Kingdom. Having sent His disciples into all the world with the good news of His kingdom, He opened wide the door to His heavenly city, where those who believe are ushered out of the darkness of one kingdom, and into the light of the eternal one that can never be destroyed.

Jesus ushered in a new age, and brought with Him, the observable kingdom of God through His mighty works. He taught the people that the kingdom is not limited to some geographical location. It is to be in them, a spiritual kingdom that abides within the believer, and that is made visible by their words and deeds.

To accomplish these things, the covenant with Abraham and the Law of Moses would have to be fulfilled and then replaced. Jesus fulfilled all the words and deeds that the Law required and that the Prophets foretold.

The old covenant with its laws and statues, and required sacrifices, and feasts *was over. A new and better covenant* was now in place. And the message of God to the Jewish leaders was that the old was done and the new had come.

The Summary

They were to exchange the constant sacrifice of animal blood in a man-made Temple, for the blood of the eternal sacrifice of the Son of God, and become the Temple of the Holy Spirit. But they refused and delighted more in the works of their own hands and their own self-righteousness.

They became enemies of their Messiah and those who believed in Him. They preferred the model of the heavenly things over the real thing; and sewing together the torn veil, they continued their religion without God. In His great love and mercy, Jesus wept over them and the destruction that would come upon them and their children, in the forty years that followed His resurrection.

Those last days brought a great advancement of the Church; with much persecution by the Jewish and Roman leaders. It was during this persecution that the Apostle John was exiled on the isle of Patmos; where he received, in a series of visions, a visitation from Jesus, who instructed him to write to the churches, and warn them of things that were about to come upon the land. Those events had both a spiritual and physical fulfillment.

Soon after the writing of the *Book of Revelation*, the Church went through a three and one-half year period of great persecution, as the devil (using the Jewish religious leaders and the Roman authorities) attempted to stamp out the work of God. These wicked "beasts" were overcome as they turned on one another.

Caesar Nero declared war against the Jews; resulting in his death and the destruction of the city of Jerusalem and the Temple. The unseen spiritual works that John beheld in his visit to heaven played out on earth in the three and one-half year struggle between the Romans and the Jews.

At the conclusion of the revelation, John sees the fulfillment of all things; culminating in the return of the Lord, the resurrection of the dead, and the completed spiritual Temple called the New Jerusalem. It is a city that shines with the glory of God, and never again will anything enter this eternal kingdom that would defile it or bring shame or pain. All tears and sorrow, every curse, and all fears will exist no more. The old is passed away and the new is here to stay.

In this study, we have primarily looked at *Matthew 24* and the *Book of Revelation* to understand what has happened in centuries past; as well as what to expect in the future ahead. We have also considered historical events that many may have ignored or were simply unaware of. But these are valuable references to better understand the meanings of the signs and symbols these Scriptures present.

I know there are many opinions of renowned scholars, whose understanding of these "end time" events vary greatly. I have had many people say to me, "Well, why does it really matter, because in the end we win?"Although this statement is true, I believe it greatly matters!

Through the centuries, people have used this (now) very common saying, "The signs of the return of the Lord are all around us; Jesus is coming back soon." They are referring to the signs Jesus gave to those in His generation. Those signs were about the great tribulation and the events found in the *Book of Revelation*; concerning global disasters and scary monsters bringing untold hardship as the devil overcomes the Church of Jesus Christ. I don't believe that these are the "signs of the times." On the contrary, I believe that our future is bright.

If your world view is that the devil is taking over, and we need Jesus to hurry back on a rescue mission to save us from the

The Summary

world and the devil; then you will most likely follow the actions of the Church over the past few centuries. Instead of being salt and light to the world, we have withdrawn within the walls of church buildings. We have "come out from among them" only to isolate ourselves by being separate from the people of the world that we have been sent to rescue.

We are not to act like the world, but we have been sent into all the world. This means that every facet of society needs your anointing and gifting operating, to transform the nations. You, believer, are needed in politics and finances, education and science, and entertainment and the arts. You carry a gifting and anointing for the purpose of fulfilling your assignment and destiny that is purposed by God.

Can you perceive a world that the prophets foretold of, where the kings of the nations will come to the Church and say, "teach us His ways that we can walk in His paths?" How about a world where they take their military budgets and use them for harvest instead of war?

I believe that we need to make long-term plans for centuries to come; not hide in our bunkers and hope for the best. The promise is that the knowledge of the glory of the Lord will cover all the earth, as the waters cover the seas. That time is still ahead of us. Are we going to be the generation that sees these things come about? Maybe not, but future generations will reap what we have planted, and will build upon all that we have built.

Friend, it is my greatest prayer "in that day," that you and your descendants will know God personally; be as numerous as the stars, abundantly blessed, and that the LORD will continue to be exalted and glorified through the mighty and matchless name of Jesus Christ working in and through the hearts and lives of all who call Him "LORD."

Other books by Dr. Dan Coflin

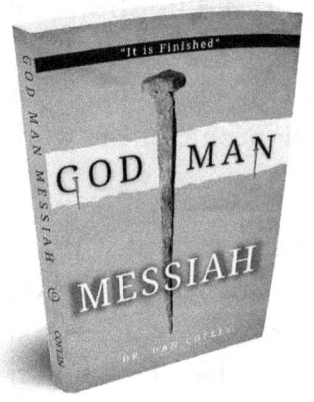

A study of the Gospels revealing the life, ministry and Lordship of Jesus Christ of Nazareth.

The purpose of this book is to reveal to you why God is good, and how the extent of His love for you exceeds anything you could ever imagine.

A daily devotional designed to gather a busy family before each member hurries off to begin their day.

To place an order, please visit:
coflinpublishing.com

www.ingramcontent.com/pod-product-compliance
Lightning Source LLC
Chambersburg PA
CBHW070559010526
44118CB00012B/1378